RUNNING YOUR OWN SHOOT

RUNNING YOUR OWN SHOOT

DAVID HUDSON

SWAN·HILL
PRESS

Acknowledgements

To run a shoot is to be involved in a continuous learning process. There is always something new to observe and absorb: a fresh thought on some aspect of shoot management to be considered and filed away for future use. Since I have had no formal training or apprenticeship in gamekeeping and estate management the information in this book has been garnered by practical experience – learning by my mistakes as often as not – and by talking to, and listening to, those with more knowledge and experience than I.

Several people have helped by tutoring me in some aspect of shoot management, but more often assistance has been involuntary, though none the less welcome for that. Seeing how others, both amateur and professional, have set about organising their shoots is always interesting and can sometimes teach us how *not* to do things as well as how they should be done.

Among those who have helped me – in a positive sense, and in no particular order – are: Bert Grant and Ronald MacDonald, Donny McKay, Jimmy Bain, Bert Robertson, Jimmy Key, Cris Amos, John Read, Billy King, Jim Watson, Grahame Young, George Wadland, Dougie McMillan, Bill Bolton, Frank Pearson, Colin McKelvie, Jimmy Leslie, Kenny Houston, Bill Howlett, Dave Hepburn, Colin Organ, Wilson Young, Jock Logie and Brian Lyall. Richard MacNicol, Rognvald Taylor and John Watters of Thurso College, deserve a special mention for showing me just how valuable a proper training in keeping can be for any young man wishing to take up this most interesting and demanding of professions. I wish something of the kind had been available when I was of an age to benefit from it.

David Hudson

Copyright © 2007 David Hudson

First published in the UK in 1998
by Swan Hill Press, an imprint of Quiller Publishing Ltd
This edition 2007

British Library Cataloguing-in-Publication Data
A catalogue record for this book
is available from the British Library

ISBN 978 1 84689 011 6

Printed in Singapore by Kyodo Printing Co. (S'pore) Pte Ltd

Swan Hill Press

An imprint of Quiller Publishing Ltd
Wykey House, Wykey, Shrewsbury, SY4 1JA
Tel: 01939 261616 Fax: 01939 261606
E-mail: info@quillerbooks
Website: www.countrybooksdirect.com

Contents

Introduction to Second Edition

It is around ten years since I wrote *Running Your Own Shoot*. When I set out to update the book for the second edition my first thought was that little would have changed in that relatively short time. It was only as I worked my way through the book that I realised just how much things have altered. Not the running and management of the shoot per se: that remains much the same as it has done since rearing and releasing pheasants and partridges began to take over from wild bird shoots. The changes are largely in the rules and regulations surrounding the sport. Ten years of New Labour have seen to that.

Hunting with Dogs has been banned (or possibly not banned) first in Scotland and later in England and Wales; lead shot has been banned when shooting over wetlands (in Scotland) or when shooting wildfowl and waders (in England and Wales); owning a pistol has been banned; burying a carcass for a midden trap has been banned; having a smoke in the lunch hut has been banned and we can no longer treat our poults with Emtryl or our rabbits with Cymag. There are moves afoot to ban rearing of pheasants and partridges, or to restrict the numbers that can be released. The cost of rearing game birds has risen, largely due to the ban on Emtryl, the whole system of farm and woodland grants has been changed and controls on the purchase, storage and use of guns and ammunition have become even more Draconian and promise to become tighter still in the near future.

Apart from that . . .

There is though, still great satisfaction to be found in planning, organising, arranging and actually carrying out all the work required in order to run a shoot. I can still rear and release pheasants and partridges, control vermin, improve the habitat on my shoot and enjoy a day in the fields and woods with my dogs and gun. Hopefully I will be able to continue to do so for at least another ten years.

Introduction

The sport of shooting has been around for a long time. From the time that man first took a pinch of villainous saltpetre and used it to blow some form of projectile out of a tube the gun has been used as a provider of meat as well as a weapon of war. No doubt it was considered a retrograde step by many at the time it first appeared – a new-fangled fad that would never replace the bow and arrow – but the advantages of gunpowder over yew wood will quickly have convinced all but the most die-hard traditionalists that the gun was here to stay. At some stage shooting game came to be seen as a suitable pastime for the gentry rather than a chore for the artisan huntsman, and from that beginning the present day sport of shooting has evolved.

That evolution has not been a steady progress. Technical and social change have both contributed, perhaps never more so than when the breech-loading shotgun replaced the muzzle-loader and opened the door to driven game shooting on a grand scale. That change was sudden and direct; more recent changes have been slower and incidental, but no less significant. Changes in agricultural and forestry practices have had an enormous effect on the habitat available for game birds and, in general, the effect has been bad. Land where once partridges, hares, snipe, plovers, corncrakes, blackgame and grouse were found in abundance may now support little or no wild game without some considerable input from man to improve the odds in favour of their survival.

For example a century ago, under what was then the normal agricultural practice, partridges thrived. Small fields, a variety of crops, well-maintained hedgerows, and an abundance of insects and seed-bearing plants meant that the grey partridge had everything necessary to flourish in the countryside. Today, in perhaps the majority of the country, partridges are scarce, even where shooting is still a major factor in the pattern of land use. There are many farms which do still hold good numbers of partridges, either because the land and the manner in which it is farmed is particularly suitable for them, or because a conscious effort has been made to re-create at least some of the conditions that so favoured them only a few years ago.

In fairness, those favourable conditions to which many shoot organisers look back with longing were also almost entirely the result of man's interference with the natural order of things. The vast majority of Britain was once covered with forest, and would be still if man had not taken a hand – and an axe – and hacked out clearings to grow his crops. From a preponderance of woodland with scattered clear spaces devoted to agriculture the land was gradually changed to the current situation: vast areas devoted to agriculture dotted with scattered areas of woodland. Birds like the partridge, which favour open fields over forests, would have gained the ascendancy as the trees retreated and the woodland birds lost their habitat. Now it is not so much a change in the basic habitat that is threatening the partridge – and hundreds of other birds and animals – as changes in the way in which that habitat is managed.

Shoot managers and gamekeepers are probably most sensitive to such changes in the local environment, if only because they have documentary evidence, in the form of game records, of the variations in population of the birds and animals which are found on their land. Birdwatchers, amateur naturalists, farmers, foresters and hikers may be aware that there are fewer skylarks, fewer curlews and peewits, fewer hares and red squirrels, perhaps more crows and foxes, not to mention more of certain introduced species such as grey squirrels and the mink, but this awareness may be no more than a vague realisation of change, a feeling that there are not as many larks exulting in the spring sunshine or peewits swooping and tumbling above the fields.

By contrast, shoot records may quantify exactly how one creature has declined while another has thrived. Estates where thousands of partridges were shot every season at the beginning of this century may now rarely make an entry in the 'Partridge' column of the game book, if at all. There will be a myriad of inter-related reasons for the slump, not all directly concerned with changes in agricultural practice. Two world wars saw thousands of keepers leaving the land to serve in the armed forces, and of those that survived the horror not all returned to the keepering profession. Death duties and inflationary pressures have caused the break-up of many great sporting estates. The creeping sprawl of towns and cities and the spread of the motorway networks has made many a shoot non-

Pheasants form the backbone of thousands of shoots, both large and small.

viable, while social pressure, often from those with no knowledge or understanding of the countryside, is a current threat to all field sports. Even so, when the game returns of shoots all over the country are taken together, a pattern will emerge which allows those with a penchant for, and an interest in, statistics to draw valuable and relevant conclusions which may eventually help us to find ways to undo some of the damage done over the past years.

It is fashionable today for shooting, hunting, coursing and other country sports including fishing, to be presented by much of the media as cruel and anachronistic pastimes which should be banned 'for the good of the countryside'. The 'cuddly bunny' syndrome pervades newspapers, television and magazines and a great deal of nonsense is written, circulated and, unfortunately, accepted as fact, by many urban dwellers who know no better. Whatever the motivation of the 'anti' brigade, be it sentimentality, class warfare or simply ignorance of the reality of life in the countryside, their message is pervasive, strident and often very professionally presented – even though it may not be based on fact. If we are to continue to enjoy shooting as a sport it may not be enough simply to take part, we may also have to be prepared to defend it vigorously against the pressures that threaten it.

The preservation of shooting – and other country sports – is important for more than the purely selfish reason of wishing to continue to enjoy a recreation that has occupied me, for one, for almost the whole of my life. Shoot management, as we shall see in later chapters, does an enormous amount to preserve and protect the countryside. Those who may not wish to shoot, hunt or fish themselves can still enjoy the benefits which accrue from the sensible and sympathetic approach to land management typified by field-sports enthusiasts. More importantly, when we set out to improve conditions for game birds, we will automatically be improving conditions for many other species, including those skylarks, peewits, curlews and the rest. They may only benefit incidentally, but any benefit is surely welcome, whatever your views may be on the subject of field sports.

Shooting is generally considered as a traditional country sport, and to a large extent that perception is accurate. The aims of the sporting shot have changed little over the past couple of centuries. Shooting means time spent out in the countryside with dog and gun, satisfying the basic hunting instinct that lurks somewhere beneath the surface in all of us – although in some of us it is rather nearer the surface than in others. The aim is not simply to kill something, although killing quickly and cleanly is certainly an essential element of game shooting, but so to arrange matters that the hunter's fieldcraft and skill with his weapons is tested – which often means that the quarry has a better than even chance of escaping unscathed. If shooting were too easy it would lose much – probably most – of its appeal. A high pheasant curling across the wind is a far harder, and ultimately more interesting, mark than the same pheasant rising from under your feet and offering a simple down-the-line-type shot. An October grouse springing 40 yards ahead of the pointing dog and skimming low across the heather is a far better sporting proposition than that same bird rising from right under your feet on the Twelfth of August.

There is a strange dichotomy in a sport where the objectives of a day in the field are both to shoot pheasants and to make those pheasants as difficult to shoot as possible. As a keeper I am delighted to see my birds rocketing high above the treetops and gliding over the guns looking like sparrows, yet I will be disappointed if they report nothing to pick at the end of the drive. As a gun I will be inordinately delighted at the one high curler which happens to fly into the shot pattern while refusing to shoot at the 'easy' low birds which

fly past at 20 feet – even though my reason for being there is to shoot pheasants and I would certainly kill more of those low birds than I would high ones. Shooting, fishing, coursing and hunting are all similar in this respect. The aim is to shoot, hook or run down a quarry, but the sport is structured so that it is not easy to achieve that aim. After all, if we simply wanted to kill pheasants we could rear them in a chicken house and shoot them through the windows.

Although shooting has stuck to its traditions in the essentials, it has changed greatly in some other respects. The partridge shoots of the eighteenth and nineteenth centuries relied mostly on the wild birds which lived naturally – or more or less naturally – within their boundaries. Gamekeepers were employed to control vermin and to protect the birds from poachers, but it was down to the partridges themselves to take care of production. Certainly they might get a certain amount of human assistance, even to the extent of having their eggs replaced with wooden dummies while the hen was sitting so that the real eggs could be incubated artificially and replaced in the nest as they began to hatch. Even so, the amount of sport that could be enjoyed each season was largely dependent on the breeding success – or otherwise – of the wild birds.

In a good year this was fine, but not all years can be good years. A cold, wet spring, a late fall of snow or a torrential rainstorm at hatching time could mean that there were few survivors among the young of the year. A poor breeding season meant that shooting would have to be severely curtailed or else there would be a danger of killing off the parent stock and turning one bad season into the precursor of a whole series of bad years.

To many sportsmen, then as now, the fluctuations from season to season are all part of the game. In a good year you enjoy extra days' shooting: in a bad year you husband your resources and cut back on your sport in order to ensure the success of future years. For me, much of the joy of grouse shooting stems from the fact that I do not know what to

Shooting over dogs was the norm in the days before breech-loading shotguns were invented.

expect when the first pointer or setter is cast off on the Twelfth. There may be big, strong coveys scattered all across the hill. There may be nothing but a few barren pairs. We may come home with bulging gamebags cutting into our shoulders, or with nothing more than tired dogs and full cartridge belts. You hope for a good year and give thanks when you get one. When times are hard you have to accept it with good grace, and then do what you can to make the next year better. That is wild shooting, and it suits me fine, but it does not suit everybody.

You may prefer your sport to be a little more assured. You may want to set out for your day's shooting knowing that, all being well, you should end up with fifty birds in the bag, or a hundred, or perhaps a thousand. You may want to go a step further, and plan for ten of those hundred-bird days this season – and next season, and the one after that. If so you can formulate a planned programme of rearing and releasing birds that should do pretty much exactly what you require.

Note that I say 'should do' rather than 'will do', because however carefully you plan, however skilled your keepers, there is always the danger that something unforeseen may occur. Disease may decimate the birds in your release pens, gales may scatter your poults to die of cold and hunger, a forest fire might wipe out birds and coverts alike. Nothing in life is certain, but some things are more likely to occur than others, and in shooting terms, rearing and releasing is a surer route to a guaranteed bag than relying on nature.

The latter half of the nineteenth century saw the fairly rapid development of the shotgun from flintlock muzzle loader to the modern breech-loading weapon using cartridges ready packaged with powder, shot and percussion cap. Instead of spending a minute or so after each shot juggling powder horn, shot flask, ram rod and percussion caps the sportsman could now press a lever with his thumb and the barrels would hinge down to allow ejectors to flip the fired cases out over his shoulder. Two fresh cartridges would be dropped into the chambers, the stock brought up to close the breech, cocking the hammers automatically in the process, and the gun was ready to fire again in perhaps four or five seconds. And if that was not fast enough he could use two guns with a man to load for him and, in theory at least, maintain at rate of fire of twenty, thirty, perhaps even forty rounds per minute.

Once technology had made sustained rapid fire available to the sporting gun it was inevitable that some of those organising shoots would set out to take advantage of this increased capacity. Driven game shooting – what was often called a *battue* – surged in popularity and almost inevitably the whole thing was taken to excess. Shoots vied with each other to produce larger and larger bags and to attract the rich and the famous to come and make up their shooting parties. Hundreds of birds would be shot at a single stand, thousands in the course of a day. It is easy today to look back and condemn this wholesale slaughter as wanton destruction, but it must be seen in the context of the times. A few years later the flower of Europe's youth would similarly be slaughtered in the fields of Flanders, driven towards the guns by the politicians and generals with little more regard than had been given to the pheasants and partridges of the Victorian shooting parties.

Most of the excesses – or what we now consider to be excesses – have disappeared in recent times. Some shoots do still produce large bags, but the emphasis today is much more likely to be placed on quality rather than quantity. Even so, it is difficult – and dangerous – to try to define what is, acceptable in terms of numbers of birds shot.

When I say that I would rather shoot one good, high pheasant that a dozen low flappers I suspect that most sporting shots would agree. Suppose, however, that at a particular drive I had the chance to shoot a dozen good, high pheasants and, unlikely though it is, I managed to kill the lot. Is that still acceptable? Let us take this a stage further and say that I was one of ten guns shooting at that drive, and that we all managed to drop a dozen of those good, high birds. And then assume that this was one of ten drives making up our shooting day, and that all ten were similarly productive. That adds up to 1,200 birds for the day's shooting. Is that a reasonable, acceptable and sporting day?

I am not going to try and answer the question, because I do not believe there is a correct response which would match every circumstance. Some shots would consider that the chance of a thousand-plus day with high-quality driven pheasants was the answer to a dream; others might feel that to shoot that many birds in a day was totally beyond the bounds of acceptable shooting behaviour. What size of bag is acceptable? It would be illogical to maintain that it is acceptable to shoot one pheasant but unsporting to shoot two. By the same logic, if one concedes that a hundred-bird day is a sporting proposition, can one justifiably condemn those who wish to shoot a thousand? In the end, the number of birds you shoot is an individual decision for each shoot manager or possibly a collective one for the syndicate.

There are certain exceptions to this general proposition. If you are fortunate enough to own a grouse moor, and even more fortunate in enjoying an exceptionally good year for grouse, it may be advisable – even essential – to shoot the grouse hard enough to bring the numbers down to a level which the winter feeding on the moor can support. If you leave too large a stock because you under-shoot then there is every chance that nature, probably in the form of the strongyle worm, will reduce your surplus population for you. In this respect nature is a less kind husbandman than the average shoot organiser, and you may well find that your grouse are reduced to next to nothing and your sport is ruined for the following years.

It can, of course, be argued that a moor which carries a stock of grouse of sufficient density to threaten their own survival will only do so if the carrying capacity of the moor has been increased artificially by man in the form of heather burning, predator control and perhaps the provision of grit, dew ponds and the like. The fact that the balance of nature (in so far as there is such a thing) has been tipped in one direction by man may mean that only further intervention will serve to prevent a disaster, at least as far as the survival of a particular species is concerned. Whether such a disaster would occur when the overstocked grouse began to die, or when the viable population was encouraged to increase beyond the holding capacity of the moor is a matter of opinion. If man is the main or only predator then you must ensure that your predation is sufficient to hold the prey population within acceptable limits. To create conditions that encourage the grouse population to explode without taking steps to hold that population within the bounds of the moor to carry them is to invite nature to remedy matters of its own accord.

For most of us, however, a grouse moor stocked with more grouse than we can manage to shoot is a problem that is never likely to cause us a sleepless night. If you are so singularly unfortunate as to find yourself in this situation then please contact me and I will be only too willing to come along with the pointers and the gun and do everything in my power to help you out!

But let us return to reality. Shooting has changed, and changed radically, since the time when wild partridges formed the backbone of shoots throughout the country. The pheasant has long since replaced the partridge as the mainstay of most low-ground shoots. Pheasants are an altogether more manageable bird than their smaller cousins. They can be produced by the hundred, by the thousand, or by the tens of thousands on game farms, and then turned down on the shoot using release pens and encouraged by the provision of food and shelter in the appropriate places to be ready and waiting for the beaters and guns come shoot day. True, the same thing can be done with partridges - with certain reservations – but it is the pheasant that is far and away the most common game bird to feature on rear-and-release shoots.

It is possible that the ease with which pheasants can be produced was a secondary factor

Hunting out a pheasant with a German pointer in a field of turnips.

in the decline of the partridge. Shooting has been an important economic and social aspect of country life for the past 250 years. If the pheasant had not been available to take the place of the partridge as the main quarry of low-ground shoots then more attention might have been paid to the plight of the partridge and the underlying causes. This in turn might have prevented a great deal of the damage to the environment that occurred with the proliferation of herbicidal and insecticidal chemicals in the past forty years, not to mention the damage to the landscape which accompanied the so-called 'progress' made in agricultural practice since the Second World War. Sadly, nothing we can do can alter what has happened, although there is a great deal that can be done to repair the worst of the damage.

Shooting has become increasingly available across the social spectrum in recent years. In the village where I grew up, pheasant shooting was very much a sport for the gentry.

The working man – and before you point out that his lordship probably worked at least as hard as most of the men he employed, I use the expression here to mean what were then called labourers, or manual workers – was unlikely to have any involvement with the shoot other than as a beater. I did not aspire to joining the shoot as a gun because it was simply beyond the bounds of possibility that I might ever do such a thing. Even the end-of-season shoot which was the equivalent of the modern keeper's day was organised for the tenant farmers, not for the beaters. We just got to beat. Now, driven game shooting can be made available at a cost that allows practically anyone who is sufficiently interested to take part.

Ironically, it is largely because the cost of running a shoot along the lines that were traditional half a century ago has become so high that it is possible for many other shoots to be run as low-cost undertakings. Many of the old estates have been broken up and sold off because of death duties, economic depression and the like. The old estate may have covered 10,000 acres, employed half a dozen gamekeepers, and shot three times a week throughout the season, with the shooting spread over three or four separate beats. Now perhaps the central core will have shrunk to a tenth of the former area, while the outlying ground may be owned by twenty different people. Instead of the shoot being a single entity, centrally controlled, there may now be fifteen or twenty separate shoots sharing the same ground where once a single shoot held sway.

It is extremely unlikely that there will be a full-time, professional gamekeeper employed on each of the fifteen or twenty shoots. Indeed, it is entirely possible that there will not be a full-time keeper on any of them, with the probable exception of the remains of the orig-

High in the hills in pursuit of grouse with a pointer.

inal shoot. A professional keeper is an expensive animal these days, even if the actual wages paid are not exactly generous for the hours keepers have to work. Add the cost of

a vehicle, a cottage, some cartridges, a new suit every year, a couple of tons of coal, the council tax on the cottage, a share in the telephone and electricity bills and a dog allowance, and the cost of employing a keeper will make a very big hole in your shoot budget.

Let us look back a few decades to the days when keepers were employed in far greater numbers than they are today. The justification for employing a keeper then was that there was enough work to require his services. His wages, like the rest of the shoot costs, would be found out of profits made in some other part of the empire. Shooting was a leisure activity (though I doubt that it was ever described quite thus) and was something that you paid to enjoy. Today, it is quite likely that a shoot manager will need to show that the money spent on keepering staff will be recovered, with interest, from the shoot income before the accountants will approve their employment. And when we take a look at costs and returns a little later you will see that recovering the costs of a full-time keeper will mean that you need to sell an awful lot of shooting.

In many shoots, small and not so small, the aim of the members is not to make a profit, but to enjoy shooting at a price which is within their means. That price may be £200 per season, or it may be £20,000. What you will get for £20,000 is clearly going to be somewhat different from what you will get for £200, although it is worth pointing out that the amount of enjoyment you get from your shooting could be just as great from the lower-priced shoot as from the higher. The question of how you can enjoy a season's driven game shooting for as little as £200 is going to occupy us for much of the rest of this book.

Running a shoot is something that can be done at many different levels of involvement. At one end of the spectrum you may elect to do all the work yourself: rear and release your game birds, control predators, build pens and fill feeders, dig out flight ponds, organise shoot days, run the beating line – and cook the lunches as well if you can fit it in between your other duties. Alternatively, you may employ a factor who will in turn arrange for a head keeper and a number of beat keepers to deal with all that. In between there are several possible alternatives which we will be considering later.

Running a shoot can be fun. It can be an absorbing (and time-consuming) hobby which will keep you out of mischief throughout the year, not just on shoot days. It can be frustrating, expensive, contentious, occasionally dangerous and sometimes just plain hard work. The deeper your level of involvement the greater the satisfaction you will derive when things go well, and the greater your sense of achievement will be at the end of a successful day. But do beware: running a shoot *can* be fun, but there are no guarantees. You may work long and hard throughout the year only to see all your hard work ruined by some factor completely outside your control – or worse, by something that you should have and could have foreseen and prevented. That said, a lot of us are deeply involved with the running of shoots, and – mostly – get a lot of enjoyment out of our involvement. Things do not always go exactly to plan, even on the best-run shoots, but that, in some ways, is all part of the challenge.

After all, as I think we have already established, if it was too easy it would not be any fun.

1 Why DIY?

There are a number of different ways in which we could define the phrase 'running a shoot'. At one end of the scale might be the landowner who employs a keeper, or possibly a number of keepers. He will decide the broad policy of the shoot – how many birds will be released, shooting dates, guest lists and the like – and the keepers will implement that policy. Shooting may take place twice a week thoughout the season with the daily bag being numbered in hundreds and the season's total in thousands. His actual involvement with the day-to-day business of rearing and releasing, vermin control, habitat management and shoot organisation may be minimal, but there is no question that he is running a shoot.

Contrast that with the person who rents 100 acres of farmland, releases a few pheasants every summer and wanders round with his spaniel every other Saturday through the winter, sometimes alone and sometimes with a couple of friends. The bag in this case may be no more than a brace of pheasants, a couple of rabbits, a pigeon and a woodcock – and that may be a good day – but, just like the landowner, this person is also unquestionably running a shoot.

Thus 'running a shoot' could refer to the process of *enabling* a shoot to take place by securing the ground and the finance and then arranging for someone else to tackle the physical work. We might equate this with a non-executive company director who attends a dozen board meetings a year setting policy and broad objectives, but who has no real involvement in the day-to-day running of the company. To continue the analogy, the person who not only organises but also looks after the keepering side of things might be compared with a small businessperson: a self-employed builder, shopkeeper or farmer.

If you happen to fall into the first category, and employ professional keepering staff to carry out your shoot management on your behalf, then you may be more concerned to ensure that their time – and your money – is being used to best advantage than to worry about whether the poults in the Home Wood should be treated for gapes, or whether the battery of the electric fence round the main pen needs replacing. Yours is the broad picture: the details are for the keepers. If however, you are the entire keepering staff as well as the shoot manager, the shooting tenant and one of the guns, or perhaps a beater or a picker-up on shoot days, then it is precisely that sort of attention to detail that will be required of you if your shoot is to flourish. In this chapter, and the chapters which follow, I shall attempt to deal with the various facets of running a shoot from as broad a perspective as is practical, and leave it to you to decide where your particular shoot fits in between the two extremes.

There is an increasing tendency today for a shoot to be run as a business, with one of the prime objectives being to show a profit at the end of the season. While I have no objection in principle to that particular concept of shoot management, my objective here is more to help you to get value for your outlay in time and money than simply to show a surplus of income over expenditure in the shoot accounts. That said, whether your aim is sport or income, good shoot management will help you to maximise either or both.

In theory it should be possible for the shoot to run itself. You simply leave your pheasants, partridge, grouse, ducks or whatever else you have on the ground to get along with their side of the business; leave it to them to see to nesting, raising their broods and rearing them to maturity. All you would need to do would be to bring along your dog and your gun and harvest the natural surplus of game on your ground. And you may well be able to do exactly that, particularly if you shoot pigeons, rabbits, wildfowl, snipe, woodcock and the like. In the case of rabbits and pigeons your problem may be keeping their numbers within acceptable limits rather than trying to produce a shootable surplus, while for the coastal wildfowler the abundance (or scarcity) of quarry may depend on factors entirely beyond your influence. So in some cases you may be able to 'run' your shoot by doing nothing more than turn up on shoot days. In the majority of cases, however, you will not.

Leaving aside rabbits and pigeons, where part of the reason for shooting them is to try and reduce numbers to alleviate damage to crops, most shoots will allow that a 'good year' is a year when there is a greater rather than a lesser amount of game on the shoot. If your shoot is a grouse moor or a low-ground shoot relying entirely on wild game, then you will probably quantify this in terms of the amount of game shot during the season. If you are rearing and releasing pheasants, partridges or ducks then it is more likely that you will

Driven grouse shooting is arguably the best, and undoubtedly the most expensive, form of game shooting.

consider the matter in terms of the *percentage* of the released birds which end up in the game cart rather than the actual number shot. Clearly, a shoot which releases 500 poults and subsequently shoots 250 will have achieved a better return on their investment than one which releases 5,000 birds and only manages to shoot 1,000 – even though the latter has actually provided more shooting.

Note that I am not attempting to argue that more birds will automatically equate with better sport. I have spent more than one long, hot day following a pointer across several thousand acres of moorland, shot nothing whatsoever, and still come home quite happy, considering it a day well spent. It is not the number of cartridges you fire, nor the number of birds you kill, that determines the value of a shooting day; it is the amount of pleasure that you derive from it. That said, if that long day on the moor had seen me returning with five or six brace of grouse then I would probably have rated it a little higher than the blank day – provided that the dogs had worked well, the company had been agreeable and the weather had not been too unkind.

The shoot which 'runs itself' is not an entirely mythical beast. There are a number which do provide sport with only the minimum of interference from man. In general though, almost every shoot will benefit from some sort of management, be it controlling predators, improving the habitat, providing food for the game, rearing and releasing birds, minimising disturbance (both human and animal) or preventing poaching. It is very much in our nature to interfere with the natural order of things so as to tip the balance in our favour. We do not always succeed; sometimes our attempts to improve things can have precisely the opposite effect. But that does not prevent us from trying. We can always hope to learn from our mistakes.

What you can do to benefit your shoot will depend largely on the type of shoot you are running. If you have a stretch of heather moorland and want to improve the prospects for the grouse you should be burning heather, controlling foxes and crows, perhaps providing grit to aid the grouses' digestion and, possibly, looking at ways to reduce the number of sheep grazing the heather. What you will not be doing is rearing grouse, building release pens and carrying bags of grouse pellets across the moor on a daily basis. Grouse do not work that way. On the other hand, if your shoot comprises woods and farmland then you will quite likely be spending your time nursing poults from egg to adult. And while you will not have grouse on the low-ground shoot you may well decide to release a few partridge on your hill to supplement the grouse shooting, and they too will require care from egg to adult.

Running a shoot can be as easy or as hard as you like to make it. You may decide to leave the whole thing to nature and just shoot whatever game happens to be on the ground when you take the gun out. Equally you may decide to release 10,000 pheasants, 2,000 partridges and 200 ducks. You can employ a keeper to do all the work for you or you can tackle the whole thing yourself. You might form a syndicate and share the work between you (although if you are going for the 10,000 pheasant option I would strongly recommend that you employ a full-time keeper). The more you hope to get out of the shoot the more you will have to put in – in theory. In practice you may find that despite all your heather burning, predator controlling and grit providing, your grouse all die from strongylosis, while the neighbouring moor, having left everything to nature, is having a bumper year. You *may* find that, but in general the more you are prepared to put in the more you are likely to get out.

There are two obvious reasons for getting involved in the business of do-it-yourself shoot management. One – the most obvious – is cost; the other is the satisfaction to be gained from a job well done. And please note that when I talk about shoot management I am including the whole process of running a shoot, not just the organising and planning. Setting a snare for a fox, building a release pen, filling feeders, topping up drinkers, cutting rides through woodland, checking tunnel traps, collecting subscriptions, even preparing the shoot lunch if you provide such a luxury – as far as I am concerned it is all part of managing and running a shoot.

The costs are easy to compute. If you are going to employ a keeper to run the shoot you can start off your shoot budget with anything from £12,000 a year upwards in salary, plus the cost of a cottage and a vehicle and whatever other allowances you agree to provide – coal, cartridges, clothing, dog food, council tax, phone bills and the like. A good keeper will be worth every penny you pay him, and then some, but it is entirely possible that you will not have anything remotely like the £15,000–25,000 a year that a keeper will cost. Having your shoot professionally keepered may well be the best option in theory but it is rarely a practical one for the smaller shoot or shooting syndicate.

So what about the satisfaction to be found in doing the job yourself? I will allow that, when you find yourself trudging through two feet of mud with a hundredweight of wheat on your back, soaked to the skin and frozen to death as you make your way round the feeders on a wet day in December, the words 'job satisfaction' may not spring immediately to mind. And finding fifty dead poults scattered across the release pen following a nocturnal visit from a fox is not going to help you start your day with a light heart. There are a great many ups to running a shoot but by definition there must also be downs. Indeed, it is largely because the job will stretch your ingenuity (and your temper) from time to time that there is such satisfaction to be derived from it when things do go well.

Because there will also be the days when the sun shines, the trees are coated in a frosty rime and the pheasants rocket out of the wood to climb high above the guns and test even the best of shots; the days when the grouse explode out of the heather in coveys of ten and twelve or the partridges skim across the stubbles to burst over the hedge and then zoom along the line of guns. There will be the poults rushing to the feed whistle on bright, autumn mornings or the mallard dropping into the flight pond, almost unseen in the winter's dusk. On a more practical level, there will be the fact that you can enjoy eight or ten days' driven shooting in a season for less than a tenth of the cost of joining a keepered syndicate. Moreover, in addition to those eight or ten days when you are actually shooting there will be other days – many, many other days – when you will be out on the shoot, feeding poults, shooting crows, lamping foxes, cutting feed rides, even planting trees, and if your interest is in the countryside and country ways rather than simply shooting then you will have hugely extended your enjoyment of the shoot.

If you only see game from the seat of your shooting stick while waiting in a butt or at a peg then you may have little appreciation of what has been done in order to get those birds to fly across the line and provide you with your day's sport. You may not even care; although the fact that you are reading this would suggest that you have at least a theoretical interest. I would suggest, however, that the more you know about the game you are shooting and the work required to produce it, the more pleasure you will obtain from your shooting. If you have actually done the work yourself then I can promise you that there is enormous satisfaction in seeing your companions enjoying their day on the shoot, be

Pheasant shooting on a frosty morning in the Scottish Borders.

they fellow guns, beaters or pickers up.

It must be said, however, that the do-it-yourself approach to shoot management will appeal a great deal more to some guns than to others. Once you start out to release poults or to provide feed in the coverts, you have a commitment that will stretch for at least the duration of the shooting season. It is not a job that can be fitted in as and when time permits: you must make sure that you can attend to your poults, traps or feeders when *they* need your attention. If you set a trap or a snare, then you *must* inspect it at least once per day – that is the law. If you are feeding your poults by hand then you had better be sure that you are there to feed every single day, or else you may find that you have no poults left to feed. If you are the sort of person who will start off the season in a blaze of enthusiasm, then lose interest as soon as the weather turns cold and the nights get dark, then you would be better not getting involved in the first place.

Running a shoot will normally involve a certain amount of hard work. Driving posts for a release pen, humping hundredweight sacks of wheat or pellets, beating the edges of a controlled heather burn, cutting rides, fencing game crops and even just getting around the shoot on foot can involve a great deal of physical effort. On the credit side, it will help keep you reasonably fit – provided that you do not slip a disc while carrying those sacks of feed or turn an ankle when you are walking round your trap lines! Some of us actually enjoy the type of work that stretches muscles as well as minds, but there are plenty who

Walking up game alone can be as much fun as a formal, driven shooting day.

do not. If you find the very idea of tramping across a ploughed field with a sack of wheat on your shoulders enough to send you scuttling to the comfort of your armchair, then I would suggest that you are not the right person to consider running your own shoot, unless you are planning to act solely in an organising and advisory capacity.

There are plenty of keen shots around who take little or no part in the running of their shoots. It may be because they are not interested in that side of the sport, or because they lack the time to get involved. In some cases they may lack the opportunity, particularly if they live in the city and have to travel a considerable distance to reach the shoot. There are guns who shoot only as guests, or as syndicate members, on ground where the keepering is already well in hand and no further input is needed. If that is how you take your pleasure then good luck and good shooting, and you will hear no complaints from me. Indeed, there are times when I would gladly exchange the delights of do-it-yourself shoot management for a regular gun in a professionally keepered syndicate which required me to do no more than turn up once a fortnight with a gun and a dog, shoot safely and tip generously. On a black and rainy December morning such an arrangement can take on a particularly attractive hue.

Most of the time, however, there is a good deal of satisfaction to be gained from working as a do-it-yourself gamekeeper. I am lucky enough to live right in the middle of a shoot, close enough to the main release pens to carry out sacks of food on my back if necessary when the fields are waterlogged. When it comes to dogging in poults on a summer evening, or lamping for a fox on a winter night, I can be there, on the job, within

A rabbit shot and retrieved to hand from the bracken.

thirty seconds of closing the back door. If I lived 20 miles away and faced an hour's driving for every return trip to the shoot I might view the matter in a different light, but the fact remains that I get a great deal more pleasure out of our little shoot than most of the other syndicate members, simply because I am involved with it every day and therefore have a much more personal stake in it.

In many ways it is more a hobby than a job of work. The problems of running a shoot are pitched at a much more practical level than those which I normally encounter from behind the office desk, and are often a good deal more interesting to solve. Like many another aspiring shot, I became involved in this type of shoot management because that was the only way in which I could afford to go driven pheasant shooting. Now, with a good few years of amateur keepering behind me, I would choose to continue with this type of close involvement right through the shooting year, even if I could afford to take a gun in one of the posh syndicates and allow someone else to do all the work.

There is a great deal of fun to be had in running a shoot, but it is most likely to be financial considerations that first make us decide to have a go at raising a few pheasant poults or putting down the odd covey of partridges. Let us suppose that you have £300 which you can afford to spend on shooting, not including the cost of your gun, cartridges, shotgun certificate, clothes, travel and so on. You could take a let day on an established shoot along with seven other guns and shoot 100 birds between you. The cost is likely to be around £2,500 for the day – say £330 per head after taking tips into account. In return for your £330 you will get one day's sport and, all things being equal, you will shoot about a dozen pheasants. If you want to get out with the gun on any of the other 364 days in the year you will have to spend some more money.

Now let us look at another way in which you might invest that £300. Suppose you get together with fifteen or so others and pool your money to give you a combined shoot budget of £5,000 or so. Spend £1,500 on leasing the sporting rights over a stretch of farmland or forestry, another £1,500 on poults, and the rest on feeding them. Muck in together to build release pens and look after the keepering side of things and you can probably look forward to eight or ten days' shooting each season. You may not shoot any more pheasants overall than you would have done if you had spent your money on a single driven day, but you will have a lot more sport for your money. Add to those eight or ten days' driven shooting all the days when you can get out to shoot rabbits, pigeons or crows, and you will probably concede that the do-it-yourself approach offers good value for money. It does not necessarily guarantee you any more shooting, at least as far as driven pheasants are concerned. Eight guns sharing 100 birds on a let day would, if the shooting was evenly spread between the guns, shoot about a dozen birds apiece. Sixteen guns shooting 200 or so birds in the course of eight shooting days will also shoot an average of a dozen birds each, but spread over eight days instead of just one.

It is up to you to decide which alternative offers the better value for your money. You might well prefer to spend the cash on a single day's shooting – particularly if you have the wherewithal to purchase another six or seven similar days during the season. Of course, if you had that much money to spend on your shooting you could also try to find another half-dozen small syndicates and shoot on forty or fifty days each season, although they would all be small days. This approach supposes that you could spare the time for all those days out shooting, could obtain membership of all those syndicates, could also find time to do your share of the work around the feed rides and release pens and finally could so arrange matters that you were not supposed to be shooting at four different places on the same day. It might be possible, but I would suggest that it is extremely unlikely.

There are certain advantages in spreading your sport thinly. If you book a single driven day's shooting and the weather happens to be foul, then your one day out with the gun may be anything but pleasant. Or you may draw an unlucky peg and find yourself away from the action at most of the drives. Eight guns shooting 100 birds will certainly *average* about twelve birds each, but you can guarantee that one of those guns will end the day having shot twenty or perhaps thirty pheasants while another may have hardly fired the gun at all. You could find yourself in either position on your one day out. You could find that you are always lucky – or unlucky – with the draw for your peg when you are shooting every other weekend from November to January, but it is far more likely that, over the course of the season, things will more or less even out.

So far we have only looked at the number of pheasants (or possibly partridges if you happen to be releasing them instead of pheasants) that you might shoot in the course of the season. But the eight-day syndicate member will almost certainly get considerably more shooting for his money than the man who opts for a single, but larger, day. There will be pigeons, rabbits, hares, snipe, woodcock, ducks, and possibly geese, crows, magpies, jays and foxes as well as pheasants to keep you occupied during the drives, and it is possible that the rules of the syndicate will allow members to flight pigeons and walk up rabbits throughout the year in addition to the formal shoot days. Overall I would submit that joining a small do-it-yourself syndicate will provide you with a great deal more sport for your money than spending the same amount on a let day or days.

Of course, value for money may not be the overriding reason for making a decision. You may lack either the time or the desire to get involved in the day-to-day running of a shoot. But apart from the cost angle, running a shoot can be an exceptionally fascinating, physically testing and mentally stimulating hobby. If you can afford the time and are prepared to make the commitment, then I can thoroughly recommend it.

2 Costs

Let us begin with a question. Imagine that someone comes to us and announces that they would like to take up shooting. They ask, 'What will it cost?'

The question is straightforward and simple. Unfortunately, the answer is not. Indeed, before we can even begin to formulate an answer we will almost certainly have to respond with some questions of our own. What type of shooting do you want to take up? How often do you want to shoot? Where do you live? Perhaps the most important question to ask the prospective shot is 'How much do you want to spend?' There is, of course, no 'correct' answer to this particular question since it is possible to enjoy a certain amount of shooting with virtually no outlay at all, and equally possible to spend literally millions of pounds on your sport – provided that is, that you have millions to spend.

Even if you have no money at all to devote to shooting you may still be able to enjoy some sport – possibly some very good sport indeed. If you make yourself available as a beater on your local shoot you may well be rewarded with an invitation to the keeper's day

A cock pheasant. Bringing a poult to the adult stage can be both expensive and time-consuming.

at the end of the season. In addition, once the keeper has got to know and trust you, you may be allowed onto the ground to flight pigeons or bolt rabbits. If you are interested in wildfowling there are still large areas of foreshore where you can shoot for free below the high-water mark, although such places are increasingly being controlled by wildfowling clubs or taken over by conservation groups who may restrict access or ban fowling altogether. So, if you are unable to afford to pay for your shooting it is still possible to enjoy a certain amount of 'free' sport – although you may find that you have to work quite hard to earn it.

But perhaps a lack of funds is the very least of your worries. How much would you like to spend on your shooting? For a pair of best English guns; you will not see any change out of £75,000. A Range Rover to carry you around? Allow another £40,000. Add £10,000 for all the accessories – hand-crafted boots, hats, gloves, hand-knitted socks, tailored tweed suits and breathable fabric waterproofs, pigskin cartridge bags and oak and leather gun cases, hand-stitched game bag and mahogany gun cabinet – and you have already spent something like £150,000 before you fire a shot. Do you want to shoot grouse in August, move on to partridge in September and October, then driven pheasants from November to January, and shoot four or five days every week? It can all be arranged, and you could spend another £100,000 every year, and much, much more if you so desired.

And if £100,000 a year is not enough for you then you might prefer to invest a few million in a sporting estate. It could be 5,000 acres of Hampshire farmland or 50,000 acres of Highland hill. Better still, buy both and start the season with grouse in the north before returning to the south for the partridge and pheasants. You will probably have stalking on both estates, red deer in Scotland and roe in Hampshire, and if you have bought wisely, salmon and trout fishing as well. The total cost? As I have already said, 'How much do you want to spend?'

For most of us, however, the real question is more likely to be 'How much can I afford to spend?', and the answer in this case is almost inevitably somewhat below the figure at which a best pair of English shotguns and 50 square miles of the Highlands begin to become a reality. Indeed, the cost of a shotgun offers a good analogy with the cost of shooting. You can buy a perfectly serviceable, second-hand, double-barrelled twelve-bore boxlock for around £100. You can multiply that by ten and buy a nice sidelock ejector made in Spain or perhaps Japan. For £10,000 you could get something very nice indeed: perhaps a second-hand best London gun or a top-of-the-range offering from one of the better overseas makers. Treble that £10,000 and you can have the very best gun that money can buy, tailor made to fit you and regulated to shoot precisely the pattern that you specify – although you may have to wait three or four years before you take delivery. No matter, though, whether you have spent the full £30,000 or only a tiny fraction of that amount, there will be very little practical difference in the performance of the guns. The £100 boxlock will kill just as effectively as the best London gun – provided that you point it in the right direction. Of course it is true that a properly regulated and individually fitted gun will get the best out of the man behind it, and that the patterns thrown by the best gun are likely to be more even and more consistent than those produced by a cheap, factory-made one. Even so, a good shot with a cheap gun will almost certainly kill more birds than a poor shot, however expensively the poorer shot may be armed. By the same token, the more you choose to spend on your shooting the more shooting you are likely to get – but it will not necessarily be better, or more enjoyable shooting.

A hen pheasant. The cost per bird shot is likely to be from £15 to £25.

We should distinguish between the *cost* of shooting and the *price*. Generally there will be a fairly close correlation between the two, but this it is not invariably so. For example, it is not uncommon to see pigeon shooting advertised at a certain price per day – £20–50 seems to be typical. That is clearly the *price* of a day's shooting, but the *cost* is actually nothing; indeed, by keeping the pigeons off the crops there may actually be considerable benefit to the landowner over and above the cash return from the shooting. Sadly, however, pigeon shooting is not typical of all shooting, particularly in the matter of costs and prices.

If you join together with seven other guns and pay £2,500 for a let day, and shoot 100 pheasants on that day, the price of your shooting can be expressed as £25 per bird. The cost will probably also be somewhere close to that figure, but it may be somewhat less and could be very considerably more – although if the provider of the shooting is to make a profit it will hopefully be less. As with all costings, some elements of shoot costs are simple and obvious to calculate, while others may be more contentious, particularly when it comes to costing the time you may have spent working around the shoot.

Let us take as a starting point a traditional, keepered shoot. We will set it on a family-owned estate of some 1,000 acres, and we will assume that there are woods suitable for coverts and release pens and that the ground lends itself to shoot development without the need for any major capital investment. To begin with we can split our costs into logical segments.

Keepering

We will assume the keeper will work single-handed, but that he will be a full-time keeper, not a farmworker who fits in a bit of keepering in his spare time. His costs are easily calculated. Wages, including National Insurance and the like, will be anywhere from £10,000–£15,000 per year, depending on his experience and your generosity. He will require a cottage – say £3,000 per year for rent, or to compensate for the rent you could have received had you let it to a tenant instead of using it for the keeper. You will probably provide him with a vehicle, maintain it and pay for the fuel used on keepering business, and that will eat up another £3,000 or so each year. Add another £2,000 a year to cover all the incidental perks such as a tweed suit, a couple of tons of coal, the council tax on the cottage, cartridges, dog food and whatever else you may agree to supply, and you will reach a figure of between £18,000 and £25,000 per year for one keeper. Let us compromise on £20,000 and take that as a starting point for the shoot costs.

Rent

Since our example is a family-owned estate, it is possible that there will be no charge for rent. Even so, we should still take rent into account, if only as the amount that could have been obtained from a shooting tenant had the shoot not been retained by the landowners. While this is largely irrelevant if you are running the shoot for yourself it is an important aspect if the cost of the shoot is to be financed externally – perhaps by forming a syndicate of guns to share the expenses. You might elect to provide the ground rent-free in return for a gun in the shoot, in which case the rent is effectively set at the cost of syndicate membership.

The amount that a 1,000-acre shoot might fetch in rent will vary considerably, depending on its location and the potential of the ground for shoot development. I know of shoots locally where the rent is set at a nominal £100 per annum – say 10p per acre. Equally, there are other shoots, particularly those which oVer exceptional quality shooting or are near to a large centre of population, which might fetch 100 times that figure – say £10,000 annually, or £10 per acre. Any amount I suggest is going to be a compromise, and you will have to adjust your costs to take into account the rent the shoot you are interested in is likely to fetch on the open market. For the sake of simplicity, I will take a round pound per acre for this shoot, and add sporting rights rental of £1,000 per annum to our costs.

Stocking

We are going to need some game to shoot, assuming that our £1,000 has not secured us 1,000 acres of ground which is overrun with wild pheasants, partridges, hares, rabbits and ducks. If you want to tackle the whole job yourself you can start out with pheasants or partridges in a laying pen, incubate the eggs and hatch out your chicks, rear them to seven or eight weeks old and then turn the poults out into a release pen. Alternatively, you can break in at any point in the production cycle, buying in eggs and thus cutting out the need for a laying pen, buying day-old chicks and saving the trouble of incubation, or leaving the rearing to someone else and delaying your purchase until the poults are ready to release. You can even buy fully adult birds which were used in someone else's laying pens, although the supply of ex-layers is obviously limited, and their management needs to be rather different if they are to stay around long enough to play their allotted role on shoot days.

The price you will have to pay for your birds will obviously rise the further along the production cycle they are before you buy them. Eggs must be collected from the laying pens and the parent stock tended, incubators and hatchers have to be bought and maintained, day-old chicks must be housed and fed. For the sake of simplicity we will stock our shoot with pheasant poults at about eight weeks old, and we will assume that we have to pay £3 each for them. You may well be able to buy poults for less, particularly if you are buying in large numbers. On the other hand, if you have opted for partridges instead of pheasants then you may have to pay more – perhaps £3.50 to £4 per bird. More important for our calculations than the unit cost is the number of units we are going to purchase. We could put down 100 birds or more than 10,000. Again, for the sake of simplicity we will settle for 1,000 poults and pay the game farm £3,000 for them.

Food

Now that we have got the birds we are going to have to feed them. The actual cost of feeding birds will vary pretty much in line with the price of wheat. How much they will eat will depend on several factors, including how successful you are at holding them on the shoot once they start to wander off from the release pen, and how early in the season you start shooting them. If you put your poults to wood in early July and do not hold the first shoot until mid-November your feed bill will obviously be higher than if you delayed restocking until mid-August and started shooting at the beginning of October. I should add that, all other things being equal, the first regime should provide far better sport, albeit somewhat more expensive, since the birds will be older, stronger and should fly a great deal higher and faster on shoot days.

The total cost of food will also vary according to whether you started out with seven-week-old poults or day-old chicks, although the extra feed bill for those first seven weeks should be pretty much offset by the saving you made in the cost of the birds. The amount that is taken by deer, badgers, squirrels, crows, pigeons and the like can also have a very significant bearing on your food costs. However, for the sake of our calculations I am going to assume that our 1,000 birds will eat about 10 tons of feed at a total cost of £1,000.

Other Costs

Capital costs may also be involved, particularly in the building of release pens, the fencing and planting of game crops, the purchase of feeders and drinkers and the like, but I am going to ignore them in this rather rough and ready costing. We are only considering the annual running costs of the shoot for the moment: the costs of the shoot itself, of buying birds, feeding them and eventually putting them over the guns. In order to achieve the latter, you will probably need a team of beaters, plus a picker up or two to collect the game after it has been shot. Some shoots pay their beaters, some provide a meal and a drink plus a day's shooting at the end of the season. Some, I understand, actually charge pickers up for the privilege of bringing their dogs along and doing a very important job for the

The cost of pen sections, drinkers and feeders will vary widely depending on whether equipment is bought in or home-made.

shoot. I am glad to say that this rather novel practice has yet to find favour in my particular corner of Scotland, and I trust it never will. Let us assume that we are going to pay a modest team of beaters – say ten of them – £15 per person each day to come along and flush the birds over the guns. If we shoot on eight days during the season our beating team will cost us some £1,200.

We can now total our running costs for the year and have a look at what sort of value for money we might hope to get.

Keepering	£20,000
Rent	£1,000
Stocking	£3,000
Feed	£1,000
Beaters	£1,600
TOTAL	£26,600

Let us round it down to £26,000. Remember that we started out with 1,000 poults going into the release pen. If we enjoy a good year we might hope to see about half of them actually in the game bag. Therefore the 500 birds we shoot are going to cost us somewhere around £50 per head. That is extremely expensive shooting. If we have managed to persuade eight guns to join a little syndicate, paying £3,300 per head as their subscription, they may well start to look around at the let days on offer from other shoots where, typically, they could hire shooting at £20-£25 per head of game shot.

But suppose that we had released 5,000 poults instead of just 1,000. Obviously our costs are going to rise – but not all of them. The keeper's wages will not change, nor will the rent or the money we pay for beaters. Only the costs of the birds and their feed will rise five-fold. Our costs now look something like this:

Keepering	£20,000
Rent	£1,000
Stocking	£15,000
Feed	£5,000
Beaters	£1,600
TOTAL	£42,600

We will round up instead of down this time and call it £44,000 – say £5,500 apiece for our eight guns. What might they expect from this example?

Assuming the same, more than respectable, return of 50 per cent, we should be shooting 2,500 birds over our eight days' shooting. Given total costs of £44,000 that works out at £18 per bird, and now the figures start to make sense – at least in commercial terms. However, although the unit cost has now come down from £50 to £18 per bird, the cost per gun has risen considerably. The eight guns in our syndicate will have to pay almost double the subscription that they were paying in the first example, but in return they will be shooting five times as many pheasants.

There are other differences, of course. Assuming eight days' shooting each season the average day's bag will now be around 300 birds, compared with about sixty per day in the first scenario. On the face of it that is a very considerably improvement: five times the shooting in return for twice the outlay. But it assumes that the guns are all willing and able to double their expenditure, and that they would actually prefer to shoot 300 birds per day instead of sixty.

A sixty-bird day, particularly if they are good sporting birds, will probably mean that the guns will have fired anything from 200 to 300 shots between them, depending on their skill. Let us say they fire an average of thirty shots apiece. If you multiply that by five, it

Far Right:
A home-made feeder to provide wheat on demand for pheasants.

Right:
Metal mesh fixed underneath will make the birds work for their grain, and may help to prevent straying.

means that on a 300-bird day each gun will fire upwards of 150 shots, and many guns would consider that to be just too much. Certainly there are plenty of shoots where the bag may be considerably more than 300 birds per day, but it represents some pretty serious shooting in anybody's book.

That said, if you aspire to that level of shooting, and can afford to set aside somewhere in the region of £5,000 to pay for it, then this shoot represents very reasonable value for money. If the ground is suitable – and it is important that it really can hold that number of birds – you might decide to put 6,000 or 7,000 birds down instead of 5,000 – perhaps even 10,000 – and the cost per unit should continue to fall, until you realise that your single keeper cannot cope any more and you have to employ an under-keeper to assist him. I will leave you to work out the extra costs for that particular scenario, and the extra birds that you might want to put down to bring the unit cost back down to a more reasonable level, plus the extra rent because you might need more ground for all those extra birds.

Let us now consider an alternative method of developing our shoot. Instead of employing a keeper to do all the work for us, suppose that we elect to do it ourselves. We will not be overambitious, so we will limit ourselves to putting down 1,000 poults, and we will again ignore any capital costs for the sake of this example. What are our costs going to be now?

Rent	£1,000
Stocking	£3,000
Feed	£1,000
Beaters	£1,600
TOTAL	£6,600

Assuming the syndicate consists of the same eight guns the shoot will cost £800 each for the season. And assuming that we shoot 50 per cent – although that may be a little optimistic under a do-it-yourself keepering regime – we have brought your costs per bird shot down to a very respectable £12.50.

If £800 a year is still a little too much for you then you might consider extending the syndicate to sixteen members. On shoot days you can split up into two teams and take it in turns to stand and to beat. Since you no longer need the services of professional beaters you can reduce the total cost to £5,000 or just over £300 per head. And if £300 is too expensive for a full season of driven pheasant shooting, then I would suggest that perhaps you should be looking at some other way of spending your spare time.

A syndicate of sixteen members means that all the guns are, effectively, half-guns, since each will only be shooting on every other drive. Assuming the same return of 50 per cent of the released stock, each syndicate member could expect to shoot around thirty pheasants during the season, at an average cost of about £10 per bird. This figure can fluctuate considerably, depending on how successful the shoot is at holding the birds initially and at putting birds into the bag on shoot days. If the percentage return fell to 40 per cent – and this might be a more realistic figure, particularly if you are learning as you go along – then each gun would shoot 25 birds on average at a cost of £12 per head.

Clearly, the guns on this type of shoot are going to have to work a lot harder for their sport than those where the keepering and beating is all handled professionally. Equally, £300 per season compares very favourably with the £3,300 that it would cost to shoot a full gun on the keepered shoot.

You may, of course, be more than happy to spend £3,300; indeed, you may be willing to double that outlay and join the syndicate offering eight 300-bird days each season and giving full time employment to a gamekeeper. I am in no way suggesting that a small, do-it-yourself shoot is somehow superior to one which is properly and professionally keepered; it will almost certainly not be so as far as the husbandry of game and control of vermin is concerned. Rather, my point is that shooting can be made available for very little financial outlay to anyone who is prepared to put in a certain amount of physical effort towards the running of the shoot. Further, I hope to show that getting involved in a do-it-yourself shoot can be rewarding in other ways than simply counting the number of shots fired on shoot days and the number of birds in the bag by the end of the season.

The examples we have been looking at so far represent only a very few of the ways in which a shoot might be run. If you had the means and the inclination you could very easily spend in excess of £100,000 per year on a single shoot. A head keeper, two or three under-keepers, perhaps your own game farm with the appropriate staff, housing, transport and the like would quickly raise your annual outlay to six figures. You might well be putting 20,000–30,000 pheasants down, although it is also possible that you could be releasing none at all and relying entirely on wild stock to provide your sport.

A small pen used to release partridges on a hill shoot.

At the opposite extreme you could probably halve the £300 per member cost of a small syndicate shoot by doing your own rearing, perhaps putting a few less birds down, and persuading the landowner to waive the rent in return for a gun in the syndicate.

Obviously the examples we have looked at are very simplistic. Among other omissions, I have made no allowance for capital costs – items such as release pens and their associated feeders and drinkers – nor for establishing game cover strips, planting permanent cover in the form of new woodland, compensating farmers for the establishment of game habitat such as unsprayed headlands or small areas left to run wild. We will be looking at all these things in some detail later, and will consider the costs involved then.

There are, of course, any number of other scenarios that can be adopted to suit your particular ground, financial resources and general inclinations as regards shoot management. If you decide to entrust the keepering to professional hands then it is likely that the major portion of your costs will be swallowed up in labour charges; if you do the work yourself then the costs of stocking and feeding are going to take most of your budget. There is quite clearly a very big jump between the overall costs of a do-it-yourself shoot and the costs incurred when a full-time gamekeeper is employed.

You may be able to find a compromise between the two extremes. If you are running a shoot on your own land you may be able to employ someone who will combine keepering work with other duties when time allows. You may find someone who is able to work part time – perhaps a retired keeper or someone with an interest in shooting and a certain amount of time to spare when needed. It is quite common to see a rent-free cottage offered in return for part-time keepering work, and there are some keepers who freelance for a number of shoots, splitting their time between two or three syndicates and thus allowing the shoot managers to split their costs accordingly.

In theory, any arrangement that allows you to reduce your overall costs should help to provide more economical shooting. In practice this may not be the case. However good he may be, a part-time keeper is, by definition, not going to devote the same amount of effort to the shoot as a full-time person would – or should. There are exceptions: I can think of at least one part-time keeper who runs a quite excellent shoot, but he probably puts in at least as many (unpaid) hours as some full-time professional keepers. Equally, I can think of one or two fully employed keepers who actually devote very little time or effort to their profession.

Employing a keeper to work full time on your shoot will not automatically guarantee its success, nor will using voluntary labour mean it will fail. That said, a full-time keeper, provided with the necessary support should – and I emphasise *should* – make a better job of the shoot than a part-timer is able to do, simply because he will be able to devote more time and effort to the job. We are, of course, talking here about shooting on a fairly large scale: either releasing a considerable number of birds or running a large wild-bird shoot. If you are only thinking of turning out a couple of hundred pheasants onto a small farm shoot then there is unlikely to be anything like enough work to keep a full-time keeper busy throughout the year, nor is it likely that your shoot budget will run to even a part-time man's wages.

You may feel, with some justification, that I have given undue emphasis to the calculation of costs per bird and getting the maximum possible return from your investment. But I am not suggesting that any shoot, other than one which is run as a purely commercial venture, should be concerned only with costs. Shooting is first and foremost a sport, and the only valid reason for going shooting should be because you enjoy it. The fact that a gamekeeper *could* rear and release 10,000 pheasants on your ground does not mean in any way that you *should* be releasing that number of birds. You might prefer

Pheasant poults on a feed ride in late summer.

your keeper to devote his energies to encouraging the wild stock, and limit your shooting to four or five days each season with the bag numbered in tens rather than hundreds. If that is your preference, and you can afford to run the shoot that way, then I am the last person to suggest that you should do otherwise. Indeed, given the choice between standing at a peg all day shooting 100 driven pheasants, and walking round with a couple of friends and a dog or two and shooting a mixed bag of pheasants and partridges, snipe and woodcock, rabbits and pigeons, I would opt for the rough shooting every time. That, of course, is my choice; if you prefer the driven day then driven shooting is what you should pursue.

There are several ways in which you can approach the process of costing a shoot, although I would suggest that most shoots choose one of the following two methods. The first is to decide what you wish to achieve and then calculate the likely costs; the other is to decide what you are prepared to spend and then work out what you might hope to achieve. Let us apply an example of each to our hypothetical shoot.

First suppose that you have decided you would like to shoot eight driven days during November, December and January, and you would like to average around 100 birds per day. If we work on a 40 per cent return of released birds we will need to start out with 2,000 poults going to the release pen in July or August. We can estimate that those 2,000 poults will eat in the region of 20 tons of food, and assuming a price of £3 per poult, and £100 per ton for wheat plus a couple of tons of pellets at £250 per ton, we can project variable costs of £8,500. Add in the rent at £1,000 and we have a total of £9,500 for our eight days' shooting – before we start to think about any labour costs.

Labour, in the form of keepers and, to a lesser extent beaters, is what might be termed a variable fixed cost. Let me explain what I mean by this term, which is not recognised by the accountants. If employing a keeper, housing him and providing him with transport and various perks costs you £20,000 per annum, then it will still cost the same whether you release ten pheasants or 10,000. He is, in effect, a fixed cost to the shoot. However, as we have seen already, you may not employ a full-time keeper. You may have a part-time keeper, perhaps a farm worker who helps out during the busiest part of the season or you may have someone who will do the work in exchange for a gun in the shoot or for a little beer-money. You may do the work yourself, or share it out among the other members of the shoot. It will still be a fixed cost, but it can vary from £20,000 each year for professional services right down to nothing for the full do-it-yourself set-up. So there it is: fixed but variable.

If we assume that our shoot is going to employ a part-time keeper, paying him a modest £50 per week and providing him with a vehicle which will cost around £2,500 a year in petrol, maintenance and depreciation, then we can add £5,000 a year to the £9,500 allowed for poults, feed and rent, and calculate that the eight days' driven shooting will cost around £15,000 per season. You may decide to pay it all out of your own pocket, or you may want to form a syndicate of eight guns and charge each of them (plus yourself) £2,000 per season, thus running the shoot 'at cost'. You might also charge each of the other guns £2,500 and make a modest profit, or charge them £4,000-£5,000 each and try to make a living out of shoot management – always supposing that you could find eight guns willing to pay £5,000 per season to shoot their share of 800 pheasants.

You might find eight such guns, but it would be expensive shooting for them, and they could undoubtedly find a cheaper alternative which would allow them to shoot many more birds for a similar outlay. Of course, if you could offer exceptionally high birds in exceptionally beautiful countryside, perhaps combined with first-class shoot dinners, it is quite possible that you would find enough guns to fill your syndicate. The quality of shooting is, after all, a subjective judgement – in other words, if your guns *feel* that they have had value for money, then value for money they have had.

Leaving aside the question of profit for the moment, the above is a simple example of calculating the cost of providing a certain level of sport. Many shoots, however, will assess their potential from the opposite side, they will need to calculate what sport they can achieve within a fixed, and generally limited, budget.

You may be an individual with some ground of your own, or with a newly signed shooting lease in your pocket, or you may be a member of a freshly formed syndicate. In either case, we will assume that you have decided roughly how much you are able and willing to spend on your shooting each year – and need to work out how best to spend the money. The amount is not important – you might have a budget of £50 or £50,000 for the season. Of course you should get rather more sport for the latter, but the principle is the same. Let us compromise, and assume that we have £5,500 to spend after paying the rent, and not including day-to-day shooting expenses such as cartridges, clothing and the like.

In terms of shoot budgets £5,000 is not a huge amount, although it will probably repre-sent a very considerable outlay to most individuals. Clearly we are not going to be able to employ a full-time keeper, and even part-time labour will make a large dent in the budget. If the cost of a full-time keeper is £20,000 a year then our £5,000 would only serve to employ someone for around two days a week. Presumably he would have to spend those two days on vermin control or habitat management, since there would be nothing left in the budget for poults or food.

As we have already seen, the combined cost of a game-bird poult and its food for the season will be about £4. A pheasant poult will cost from £2.50 to £3, and eat about £1 of food; a partridge poult will cost a little more, but eat a little less. Suppose we decide to buy in 1,000 seven-week-old poults, and set aside £4,000 to cover their costs. They will need a release pen, or better, several release pens, hoppers for their food and drinkers for their water. This will easily absorb another £500, and that is assuming that you build the pens yourself and probably use recycled materials as far as possible. That leaves us with just £1,000 to cover all other costs.

If we are prudent we will take out third-party insurance for our shoot and keep a few pounds back as a reserve against any unforeseen emergencies. This will leave us with less than £1,000 – and we still have not paid any labour charges. For example, we might decide that we will need eight beaters on each of the eight driven shooting days we plan to hold. If we pay the going rate of £15–£20 per head then there will be nothing at all left in the budget. Alternatively, perhaps we can find a retired keeper who will look after our poults and see to feeding them through the winter as well as watching out for poachers and keeping down the vermin. If we give him £20 a week to cover the cost of his petrol and cartridges, with a little bit towards his time, then there will be no money for beaters. We can probably get free beaters in return for a brace of pheasants each and a decent keeper's day at the end of the season, so that may not be a problem.

Once we have had some experience of trying to hold and present the birds we may find that our coverts are lacking in some respect. We may need to establish a few acres of game crop around the shoot. This will mean more money for fencing, seed and cultivation, plus

some compensation to the farmer for the loss of a few acres of productive land. Alternatively, with the pens built and the feeders and drinkers all in place we might try to increase the numbers of poults we release. More poults will mean more work for the keeper, or more work for us if we are doing it all ourselves. We might be able to cope with the extra work, as might our part-time helper, but there will obviously be a point at which the extra work becomes too much.

Grouse – a strong covey flushing from the heather in early August.

Running a shoot on a fixed budget is somewhat akin to one-handed juggling. It is generally possible to reach a compromise level at which things run smoothly, but it is likely to be a fairly delicate balance. It is almost certainly better to start off with a modest target and build up slowly over several seasons until you have a real grasp of what you can, and more importantly cannot, achieve, than to charge in blindly with thousands of poults scattered through half a dozen release pens right from year one. If you cannot keep your feeders topped up or your straw rides fed, then you are likely to lose a great many of your birds through straying, and you may even end up shooting fewer birds than if you had started with a more manageable number in the first place.

The most important thing to remember about shooting, and running a shoot, is that success should be measured in terms of enjoyment, not solely in terms of unit costs and percentage returns. Certainly you should consider how efficiently you are running the operation, but at the end of a shooting day, or at the end of the season, it is whether you and your fellow guns, beaters, pickers up and amateur keepers consider that your time has been well spent that is important. If shooting becomes nothing more than a job of work or an exercise in bookkeeping, then it is probably better all round if you devote your energies to something else. There are more than enough of us who shoot purely for the enjoyment to fill the gap which you will leave behind.

3 Where to Shoot

The question of where to shoot may have no relevance for you. You may already know where your shoot will be; you may own or rent the land yourself, or have already been offered the shooting rights over some ground and be wondering how best to develop it. If so, then you have overcome the first hurdle.

On the other hand, for many people where to shoot is the first, and potentially the most important, of the many questions which must be answered before they can take their first steps towards running their own shoot. Finding somewhere to run your shoot may be absurdly easy, or it may be close to impossible. As with so many other aspects of shooting, the difference between simplicity and impossibility will hinge on two main factors: where you live and how much money you have to spend.

Grouse shooting may be expensive but there is always a good demand for it.

The second point is obvious. Given unlimited funds anyone can enjoy shooting pretty well wherever they please. I should perhaps amend that to read 'pretty much whatever *type* of shooting they please', money alone will not bring you an invitation to shoot pheasants

at Sandringham or grouse at Balmoral. You can, however, purchase shooting of the highest quality all over Britain – all over the world for that matter – if you have a cheque book to match your desires. You may not be able to buy the social kudos that some people would associate with certain shoots, but you can certainly buy shooting of at least equal quality. In the same way, if you have enough to invest you will always be able to find shoots and shooting rights for sale or lease. A shoot is a commodity much like any other, and subject to normal market pressures. No matter what you are looking for, be it driven grouse or walked-up partridge, high pheasants or flighted geese, if you can afford to pay for it then you should be able to find something to match the shoot of your dreams.

The majority of us, however, will have to dream on, pending a lottery win. Fortunately, by no means all shooting rights require large sums of money. The actual amount you will have to pay will depend on what you are buying and where you are buying it – which brings us back again to the first factor, which is where you live.

It is a simple matter of supply and demand. Running any shoot requires that you have an area of suitable land to shoot over, and land is a commodity that is in finite supply. We cannot manufacture more land to meet demand, and therefore the price of land – and land usage – rises until demand falls to match the available supply. If you live in the crowded south-east of England, for example, suitable land is likely to be in very short supply indeed, and there will be a very healthy demand for shooting from among the millions of other people in the area. On the other hand, if you live in certain parts of the north of England, Wales or Scotland, you may find that there are shooting leases going begging, simply because nobody wants to bid for them.

In theory, therefore, finding somewhere to run a shoot may present the same problems whether you are in Sussex or Sutherland, but in practice the exercise is likely to prove easier in some places than in others.

If you do not already have your shooting lease organised, then there are a number of obvious places to look for shooting for sale and to let. Magazines such as *Shooting Times*, *The Field*, *Country Life* and the *Shooting Gazette* all carry advertisements for shooting, ranging from forestry shoots which might attract a rental of a few hundred pounds per year to sporting estates which are offered for sale for a few millions. But these are all national publications, and while they might well offer shooting in your locality you should also scan the columns of your local press. Shoots and shooting rights may appear less frequently there, but those that are advertised will almost certainly be somewhere close at hand.

Most advertisements offer shooting by the day or by the season, with the purchaser buying the shooting on an established shoot. This is fine if you simply want to shoot, but if you are looking to run your own shoot then you will be looking for the shooting *rights*, rather than just a day or days out with the gun. Most advertisements will make it clear whether they are offering shooting or the shoot itself, but occasionally they can be somewhat ambivalent. 'Shooting available over 500 acres' could refer to rough shooting which is let by the day or the long-term shooting rights. Sometimes only further enquiries can clarify the matter.

The wording of the advertisement will usually give you a good guide to the cost of the shoot. The more enthusiastic the phraseology the more you are going to be asked to pay. Phrases like 'well established', 'fully keepered', 'heavily stocked' or 'magnificently laid out' all suggest that this may not be the sort of place which is best suited to a few days' rough shooting. On the other hand, an advertisement that offers 'shooting rights available over a number of areas of forestry' is promising something that should be a lot easier on the pocket initially. How much you may spend on it once the lease is established is likely to be a matter between you and your bank manager.

In between these two extremes you will find all manner of shoots available for rent or to buy. Some may be offered as going concerns with keepering staff already employed who can be taken on by the new owner or tenant, or have a keeper's house included with the shooting rights. Others may consist of nothing more than a piece of land which someone has decided may have the potential to be developed as a shoot, with the possibility of bringing extra income to the owner. You may be able to get full details of the prospects

Guns gathering between drives at a driven pheasant shoot.

by making a telephone call, but in some cases, you may be asked to pay simply to receive a brochure describing the shoot.

You can, of course, place your own advertisement in either the national or local press. Such advertisements are not uncommon, and they often emphasise the character of the advertiser, along the lines of 'safe experienced gun seeks' or 'established syndicate of responsible, professionals require'. Safety, experience, and social standing are all commonly quoted factors which the advertisers hope will persuade a prospective landlord to reply to their advertisement. Another common approach is along more mercenary lines, with advertisements which begin, 'X thousand pounds cash available in return for' or 'syndicate with ample backing seeks . . .'. I have also seen requests for shooting rights which have stressed the keepering or game management experience of the advertiser, generally because the intention is to develop a shoot along commercial lines, possibly in partnership with the landowner. If you decide to advertise, you must tailor your approach to suit your own particular circumstances. I have no idea how successful such requests for shooting are, but it is worth noting that a small ad in either your local paper or one of the national shooting magazines will cost very little, and might just result in your finding the very thing you are seeking.

Estate agents are another obvious place to ask about shooting rights. You are unlikely to get much satisfaction from the sort of agent who specialises in selling suburban semis and city flats, but the more agriculturally inclined agents deal with sporting leases as well as farms and woodlands. It may be well worth a personal visit to discuss the type of ground and shooting that you have in mind, even if the agent has nothing suitable on offer at the time. There is always a chance that the type of thing you are looking for may come up in the future, or that the agent may be able to suggest somewhere worth considering even if it is not actually on the market at the time. A couple of friends and I once managed to lease a considerable area of hill ground which was ideally suited to releasing a few partridges for shooting over dogs simply by approaching the agent and asking if any rough hill ground suitable for developing for shooting was available. It was, but it was not actively being offered for lease simply because the grouse stocks had fallen to virtually nothing because of overgrazing, and no one had considered its use for partridges. It was not expensive, but then it was not worth very much as a shooting prospect unless the tenants were prepared to put in a lot of work for a relatively small return. We were and we did, and we gradually built up a small but interesting rough shoot.

The very fact that shooting rights are offered by an estate agent or advertised in the press would suggest that the ground in question is at least basically suitable for use as a

Guns shooting in this sort of country must be prepared for quite a lot of walking.

shoot. There may already be a well-established shoot in existence, or it may be that the sporting uses of the ground have been neglected for some time. The better established the shoot the higher the price is likely to be, for obvious reasons. If you are renting ground which already carries a stock of game, has ready-made release pens, well-maintained coverts, blocks of game crop, existing feeders, perhaps even the equipment for hatching and rearing chicks, then you will clearly be expected to pay a significantly higher rent than you would for the shooting rights over land which has 'potential' but little else. This is not necessarily a drawback, since starting out with a blank canvas will allow you to build up the shoot according to your own ideas rather than simply continuing in the manner of a previous shoot manager. There is little point in paying a premium price for an 'off-the-peg' shoot if you subsequently decide to change everything around.

Shooting rights offered for tender by the Forestry Commission or by one of the privately owned forestry management companies may well be different. It is not unusual for the shooting rights over large forestry blocks to be made available to the highest bidder, even though the ground in question is almost totally useless for developing as a conventional driven shoot. A thousand acres of forest may sound an attractive prospect, but if the whole of the acreage is blanketed in serried ranks of mature Sitka spruce, then your shooting may be limited to flighting pigeons as they come in to roost at dusk. You may be perfectly happy with that, but it is as well to understand the limitations before you sign the lease – and the cheque.

Responding to an advertisement may be the conventional method of acquiring shooting rights but, by its very nature, it will place you in competition with others who are looking for a shoot of their own. While there is nothing wrong with competition, it may be difficult to convince a prospective landlord that you are the right person to be trusted with his shooting rights, particularly if you have no track record in shoot management and are competing with others who do. Besides, competition also tends to push up prices. So it may be better to try and find a suitable shooting ground before the owner or his agent offers it publicly.

Depending on where you want your shoot to be, you may have to wait for a long time before the right shoot – or one which is even nearly suitable – is advertised. Of course, if the shoot is being run on your behalf by others then the distance from your home may not be a problem, within reason, but if you intend running the shoot yourself, particularly with some measure of 'hands-on' involvement, then it is almost essential that it is somewhere close to your home. Just what is 'close' will depend on your particular circumstances. If you live in a rural area, and do not drive a car, then 'close' might be within 5 miles. But if you live in the middle of London, Birmingham or Manchester, a shoot which was within a 20–30-mile radius might be considered close to home. Only you can decide what is acceptable. Beware, however, of being over-optimistic when considering the travelling that will be involved when running your shoot. If going shooting involves a 20-mile drive once a fortnight from November to January then it is unlikely to cause any problems. However, if you have to make that same 20-mile drive every single day from July to November in order to feed and water your pheasant poults, then carry on two or three times a week until February to top up feeders or lamp for foxes, you may find that the travelling and the call on your time become unacceptable. It is one thing to spend a couple of hours driving to the shoot, feeding poults, and then driving home again on a warm evening in September, but it is quite another to make that same trip on a dark, wet

Well-presented, high pheasants will always be in demand from guns who will pay top prices for this type of sport.

November afternoon or evening, ploughing about in thick mud and then driving home soaked to the skin. If you are planning to do all the work yourself then I would advise you to think very carefully before becoming committed to a shoot which is any great distance from your home.

The amount of spare time you have available will also have a considerable bearing on where your shoot should be, and on the way in which you organise it. If you have to work normal office hours, then from the middle of November onwards it is likely that you will be at work during all the daylight hours from Monday to Friday. This will effectively prevent you from doing any work around the coverts apart from at the weekend. If you live really close to the ground you may be still be able to feed rides or check snares before leaving for work, but if you have a 40-mile round trip to make to reach the shoot then you will need a very understanding boss or extremely flexible working hours.

Of course, you may work night shifts, be self-employed or not be working for one reason or another. You may even make your living by organising shooting. If this is the case and your circumstances allow you enough free time during the daylight hours, then distance may not be a problem at all. The important point, however, is to make a realistic assessment of the time you will be able to devote to your shoot throughout the season and then consider whether it is enough to allow you to develop it in the way you want. Having your shoot close to home is not essential, but it can be a considerable help, particularly when the days become shorter and the weather grows wetter and colder.

If you are looking for ground close to your home then your local knowledge should help you to identify possible locations. Once shooting rights have been advertised, it is almost certain that there will be other parties interested besides yourself. There will be an element of competition, and in any competition there must be losers as well as a winner. So if you know your area and can find a suitable shoot and then approach the owner privately you may be able to secure a lease without the need to out-bid other parties, or to convince the owner that you are the most suitable of a number of possible tenants.

Persuading someone that you are a suitable tenant may be a bigger obstacle to obtaining shooting rights than simply finding a shoot and producing the money to pay for it. Many landowners are quite understandably reluctant to grant armed access to their land to a complete stranger. Buying a day's shooting is one thing, but a shooting lease which may run for several years is quite another. A shooting day should be very much under the control of the organiser, whereas a shooting tenant will normally have a great deal of freedom in the way he can act. A landlord will want to be satisfied that his shooting tenant will conduct shooting days safely and with an acceptable code of practice for his guns and beaters. Crops and livestock must be respected, trapping and vermin control carried out within the bounds of the law, release pens maintained in a clean and tidy condition, and any areas where the shoot may be in conflict with forestry or farming activities resolved in a manner agreeable to all parties. These are not always easy objectives to achieve. It follows then that anyone offering shooting rights for lease will want to be satisfied that a prospective tenant will not be a source of problems rather than of revenue. While a landlord can, and probably will, require some form of reference from a prospective shooting tenant, there is no doubt that most would prefer to let their shooting to someone they know and believe they can trust, rather than to a complete stranger, however good his references may be.

This brings us back to the matter of local knowledge. Before looking further afield for shooting it is always worth considering the situation close to home – assuming that 'home' is not in the middle of a city. Do you know of any farms or forestry plantations which are not currently being used for shooting? There may be a good reason why the shooting rights are not taken up, but it is just possible that there may be shooting available close at hand which could be yours simply by making an enquiry and an offer. There is an excellent little mixed shoot just across the valley from where I am sitting which was started a couple of years ago on the strength of a casual enquiry to the farmer who owns the land. He enjoyed the occasional wander about after whatever game happened to be in the fields and woods, but had neither the time nor the inclination to develop the shoot further. It was suggested that he might allow a small syndicate to take over the shooting, building release pens, putting down some pheasants and partridges and keepering the ground. In return, he would take a gun in the shoot. It has so far worked extremely well, to the satisfaction of all parties, but the arrangement came about only because of the initiative of one of the syndicate members. Had he not approached the owner with his proposal the land would simply not have come onto the shooting market.

Similarly, one of the neighbouring shoots, which covers several thousand acres of excellent terrain for driven pheasants, has recently sublet one end of their ground to a separate syndicate. It was a part of the shoot which had never been much used by the parent syndicate, simply because they had other, better drives to keep them occupied throughout the season. They might beat through those woods on an outside day for the odd pheasant which had wandered off in that direction, but in general the ground was simply ignored until they were asked to consider a sublease. Subletting makes sense for both the parties.

Hill ground shoots can provide good sport for the gun who is prepared to get out and walk, whatever the weather.

It provides shooting for the new syndicate, and it means that a part of the ground which had been pretty much neglected in the past is now properly keepered. There is a certain amount of give and take between the two syndicates as far as their released pheasants are concerned, but provided that both act reasonably any losses of birds from one syndicate to the other should be offset by corresponding gains. A subtenant who tried to take advantage of his position by drawing birds from the main shoot without releasing any of his own would quickly find that his shooting rights had been withdrawn. In many cases a shooting lease will stipulate a minimum number of birds which must be released each season, particularly if the leased shoot marches close to any shooting which is retained by the landlords.

Again, this shoot would never have been offered for rent if an approach had not been made to the parent shoot with a suggestion that the ground might be sublet to the advantage of both parties. It is unlikely that such an approach from a stranger to the area would have been successful; an essential part of the deal was that the members of the parent syndicate knew and trusted the people making the offer to sublet.

We have already seen that there may be big disadvantages in trying to run a shoot which is located too far from your home, and you may be able to use this problem to your advantage if there is a shoot near you which is run from a distance. It presents a clear opportunity for you to become involved in keepering and running the shoot in conjunction with the existing tenant. Again, you are more likely to achieve this type of arrangement if you are already known to the shooting tenant. An offer to take over the keepering from a complete stranger is likely to meet with a slightly frosty reception, but if you have previously offered your services as a beater or picker up and shown that you are competent, knowledgeable, keen and trustworthy, there is every chance that your services will be welcomed.

You may have a very clear idea of the type of shoot you wish to run, be it driven pheasants, walked-up partridges, grouse over bird dogs, pigeons over decoys or rough shooting for whatever might turn up on the day. If so, then you probably also have a very clear idea of the type of ground you want. Some types of shooting require very specific terrain – you will not shoot many grouse, for example, unless your shoot includes heather moorland – while other types, such as driven pheasant shooting, can be run successfully over a wide variety of countryside. It is true that it will generally be easier to show high pheasants when your shoot is in hilly country than if it is somewhere in the fens, but if you happen to live in the fens and are looking for somewhere close to home to run your shoot then you will have to be satisfied with flat terrain.

If you are clear about the type of shoot you intend to run, and the type of terrain you need to run it, then you will be able to assess any ground that is available on a reasonably objective basis. However, you may prefer to approach the problem from a different angle and look at what ground is available with a view to assessing the best way of developing it as a shoot. But while this is a more flexible approach and should increase the scope of your search for suitable ground it is only of use if you yourself are prepared to be flexible in your approach to shooting. While I am perfectly happy to spend the whole day trailing around behind a pointer or setter in the hope of shooting two or three partridges, I am well aware that a six-hour tramp across broken hill ground is not an attractive prospect to every sportsman. If you want to shoot several hundred cartridges in the course of a day, break for a three-course lunch between 12 and 2 o'clock, and never have to stroll more

Since grouse cannot be reared artificially great care must be taken to avoid overshooting.

than 50 yards from your Range Rover, then the sort of rough hill ground that will hold the odd covey of partridge or grouse is never going to form the basis of your ideal shoot. I am not in any way critical of this preference, since I am more than happy to shoot driven pheasants myself when the opportunity arises. I am merely pointing out that a piece of ground that might be ideal for one person could be little better than useless to another.

The fact that the ground you have found is not immediately suited to your plans may not be an insuperable problem. You can adapt your plans to suit the type of ground which is available, or you can try and adapt the ground to suit your requirements. What you can do will depend to a great extent on the existing land usage and the extent to which changes can be made to accommodate the shoot. Game-holding cover can be produced very quickly by sowing some of the various mixtures of game crop which are available, set-aside ground can be planned so as to encourage game birds to nest, crop rotation can be organised for the benefit of the shoot, odd corners can be left uncultivated to provide habitat for game birds.

There are dozens of things which *can* be done to improve land for shooting purposes; the problem for the shoot manager is likely to be whether those with other interests in the land are able or willing to make the necessary changes. It is one thing for a landowner to agree to allow you sporting access to his land, but it is quite another for him to make wholesale changes to the way he runs his business in order to improve your shooting. If planting blocks of game cover, establishing conservation headlands and making changes in the set-aside scheme are essential to your plans for game production then you must

The degree to which driven pheasant shooting can be developed is very much under the control of the shoot organiser.

make sure that these changes are acceptable to the owner of the ground (and to the farming tenant if there is one) *before* you sign the lease. You should, of course, expect to pay compensation for any loss of income that the farmer may suffer as a result of taking land out of agricultural production. If he agrees to your planting an acre of game crop then you should be willing to pay him for the income that acre of ground would otherwise have earned – unless, of course, this arrangement is already covered in your agreement.

Even with the willing assistance of all concerned it may still not be possible to turn the ground which you have available into the type of shoot you want. If you are trying to provide cover for pheasants on rough upland grazing you may have to accept that there are certain types of game crop which will simply not grow, under any circumstances, in that particular situation. Even if you succeed in producing a suitable crop, your pheasants may still vote with their feet and take themselves off to ground which they consider more suited to their needs. If you started the season with a couple of hundred poults and an open mind, then such a misfortune may be little more than a useful lesson for you. If, however, you started out with several thousand poults and a dozen days' shooting commercially let, then a mass migration of your stock could mean financial ruin. Experiment by all means, but do consider the implications of failure as well as the rewards of success when planning the experiment.

You will always be best advised to work with rather than against nature. If you are taking over an existing shoot the game records will give you a good idea of what has been achieved in the past. If the shoot is a grouse moor, then bag records are a good indication of the potential of the ground, although you must take into account the level of shooting pressure which has been maintained in order to achieve those bags. If the moor has been lightly shot then taking a heavier crop might even be beneficial to the stocks. But beware of a moor which is offered for lease following a sudden rise in the bags over the past year or two. Such a rise might indicate that grouse stocks are improving, but it might also be indicative of a couple of seasons' deliberate overshooting in order to boost the price when the moor is offered for let.

Working with nature means not trying to force huge numbers of pheasants onto ground which does not have sufficient cover to hold them, or trying to rear hundreds of ducks on a pond which is only suitable for a couple of dozen. Almost every shoot will aim to raise and maintain game stocks at a higher than natural level, in order that there is a surplus of game to be culled. In many cases the wild stock will be artificially boosted by rearing and releasing birds, and on many shoots practically all the game will be produced in the rearing field rather than in the wild. There has been a great deal of debate and not a little condemnation in recent years of shoots which release too many birds. You may like to try and define the point at which rearing and releasing game ceases to be an acceptable way of enhancing the shoot and becomes simply a production line churning out live targets, but personally I am loathe to try and quantify it. There is no clear dividing line between the acceptable and the unacceptable face of shooting. Rather it is a matter for the individual shoot and for that difficult-to-define quality of 'sportsmanship'.

For myself, the wilder the sport and the greater the element of hunting involved the more I enjoy it. I much prefer shooting grouse over pointing dogs to shooting driven pheasants, and I would rather shoot one wild duck than a dozen which have been reared. That said, I would agree that there would be precious little shooting available if we all had to rely solely on wild game. If you control a shoot which has the right elements to allow a shootable surplus of truly wild game to be produced then you are very lucky. Most shoots have to rely on reared and released birds to produce that shootable surplus. Provided that you set about releasing and showing your birds in the most sporting manner possible for your particular circumstances, I can see no problem.

Finding suitable ground can be the most difficult part of setting up and running a shoot. If you live in an area where shooting rights are regularly offered for lease or sale then you can enjoy the luxury of picking and choosing until exactly the right ground is available. If, however, you are forced to snatch at whatever crumbs are available then you may need to adopt a more flexible attitude and adapt your ambitions to what is on offer. As we will see in later chapters, there is a great deal that can be done to turn even the most unlikely ground into a rewarding and interesting shoot. All it requires is a little ingenuity, a lot of determination, and a great deal of hard work.

Heading for home at the end of the day. There is a lot more to be gained from shooting than simply financial returns.

4 What to Shoot

Let us assume that the question of where your shoot will be situated has been answered, and that you have either already secured the shooting rights over a suitable piece of countryside or are looking at a piece of ground with a view to making an offer. You may be considering 50 acres of waste ground on the edge of a city, 500 acres of mixed farmland, 1,000 acres of forestry plantation, 5,000 acres of heather moorland or a combination. It may be a little less than the 50 acres in total, or it may be a lot more than 5,000. When you have got the ground, the next question is what you are going to do with it.

In some cases that question may be irrelevant. If you have just taken over an existing driven pheasant shoot, complete with rearing fields and release pens, well-established drives, shoot vehicles, feed hoppers and a full team of keepers, then you should already have a pretty good idea of what the next season will bring. If your new shoot happens to be a grouse moor then your main interest is likely to centre around the existing grouse stock and the prospects for the next breeding season rather than where to build a release pen and how many pheasant poults to order from the game farm. Equally, you may have taken on the new shoot for the specific purpose of creating a particular type of sport, be it driven pheasants, walked-up partridges or duck flighted into ponds at dawn and dusk. However, in some cases, you will just be happy to have secured some shooting – any shooting at all – and will be wanting to inspect the new ground with a view to assessing its potential.

Pheasants and chicks, the most common and widely distributed of game birds.

There are two ways to approach this. If you have taken on the ground with the intention of running a particular kind of shoot, then you will obviously be looking at how well the existing pattern of land usage will meld in with your plans, and what changes may be needed to improve things in the future. If you have taken on the shoot for a specific purpose, you will hopefully already have satisfied yourself that it is basically suitable for what you plan to do, but you may have simply grasped the chance to lease whatever was available. Or you may already control the shooting rights as the owner of the land and be looking for ways to develop your ground for sporting purposes. In either case, I would suggest that you approach the matter with an open mind and assess its potential for various types of game and shooting before deciding how best to proceed. Let us begin by considering the requirements of the main sporting species.

Pheasants

The pheasant is the mainstay of the great majority of shoots. Despite being the most common of our game birds, it is not a native of these islands, having its origins in the swamps and jungles of Burma, China, Japan, Mongolia and other parts of Asia. It may have been brought here by the Romans, and has certainly been well established since Norman times, so it is perhaps a little unfair to class it as an in-comer; even in the more rural corners of Suffolk a family which has lived there since the days of the Conquerer would be considered as locals – just.

The pheasant is, above all, adaptable. Despite being a native of the Far East, it will live quite happily on the flat, windswept fens of East Anglia or in the steep, wooded gullies of the West Country. You can find a pheasant almost anywhere: in the wide, open, green seas of a sugar-beet field or on a rocky Welsh bank among the bracken; in wet, reedy marshlands or on dry, chalky downs. It will eat almost anything it can stuff into its beak, roost high up in a fir tree or sleep jugged down on the ground, build its nest in a wood, under a hedgerow, in a road-side verge or out in the middle of an open field. It will live a solitary life on a gorse-covered hillside or cohabit happily with a thousand others in a release pen. Temperamental it is not.

An experienced keeper can manage his pheasants almost as if they were domestic poultry. They will come running to a whistle to get their morning feed and fly along a predictable path when flushed by a line of beaters. They will also hurl themselves under passing cars with suicidal abandon, build nests in places where they are certain to be discovered by any passing dog, cat, fox or badger, and lead any chicks which they do hatch through streams and ditches which will drown them. Versatile and adaptable as they are, they can also be quite unpredictable, and may suddenly decide to wander off beyond the boundaries of your shoot for no apparent reason.

Because of their catholic tastes it is possible to establish a pheasant shoot almost anywhere where there is a modicum of cover; the tops of mountains and the more open stretches of bogs and moorlands being obvious exceptions. By choice the pheasant is a bird of the woodland margins, with a preference for open fields for feeding and sunning, with nearby woodland for roosting and sheltering from the weather. Warm woods with plenty of ground cover beneath the trees are preferred to cold, open plantations, although they will happily scratch about in the leaf litter under beech trees in search of beech mast and insects.

A hen pheasant flushed from rough cover heads for the safety of the trees . . .

. . . But is soon brought to hand by this gun's golden retriever.

Where there is a lack of suitable woodland cover, habitat for pheasants can easily be established by planting game crop – various mixtures of food and cover plants which can be chosen to suit your particular soil type and weather conditions. Farming practices can be adapted to benefit pheasants and other game birds, often with no detriment to farm profits. The very ease with which pheasant shooting can be established has sometimes led to what is seen as the unacceptable face of shooting, where huge numbers of birds are concentrated on ground which is patently unsuitable for them. That said, building a release pen and ordering 100, or 1,000, pheasant poults will not automatically guarantee you a season's sport. Pheasants may be easier than most of the other game birds when it comes to rearing and releasing, but there are still plenty of things which can go wrong when you embark on your stocking programme.

Partridges

The partridge was once the main low-ground game bird, but it has gradually been supplanted by the pheasant. There are two varieties: the native grey or English partridge and the rather more gaudy red-legged or French partridge. A combination of changes in farming methods, the increasing use of pesticides, the rising cost of gamekeepers' wages and the fact that pheasants provided an easier alternative for driven shooting saw partridge numbers fall drastically in the latter half of this century, although there are encouraging signs that more shoots are now seeking to produce partridges as well as, or even instead of, pheasants.

The partridge, English or French, likes to make its home in the open, on farmland, downs, heaths, low moorland and rough pasture. In the days when farms were made up of small fields surrounded by hedgerows, with a variety of crops being grown and stubbles left through the autumn awaiting the plough, the partridge thrived. It was the sudden destruction of so much of our countryside after the Second World War, when successive governments encouraged farmers to grub out hedgerows, soak their crops in herbicides and pesticides, concentrate on vast monocultures of barley or beet and drain, lime, plough or reseed every available scrap of land, that hurried the demise of the partridge, along incidentally, with most of our other ground-nesting birds.

Nevertheless, a more sympathetic approach to farming, the sensible use of set-aside options and some slight restraint with the sprayer can do a great deal to restore the land to the point at which the partridge again becomes a viable alternative to the pheasant. Tight control of vermin, particularly foxes and crows, will do much to assist any wild partridges which are on the shoot to rear their young successfully, while simple techniques for releasing partridge poults have been developed in recent years which make restocking a possibility for most low-ground shoots. Partridges make an interesting addition to pheasants, particularly since their season opens at least a month earlier. The First of September used to be as significant a date in the shooting man's calendar as the Twelfth of August, and for many shoots it is becoming so again. For the majority of driven pheasant shoots which will not begin their shooting until late October or early November, a modest investment in partridges can extend the season by two months and provide shooting during the best of the autumn weather.

If your new shoot runs over the kind of marginal moorland that is too exposed for pheasants and too rough and grassy for grouse it is well worth considering releasing partridges rather than trying to persuade pheasants to settle on ground which is really not suitable for them. They are tough, self-reliant little birds, and can be far more sporting than pheasants, particularly when they have been exposed to gunfire a couple of times. They will thrive on the roughest of rough grazing, provided that you phase their release properly, and will settle down on ground where holding pheasants would be almost impossible.

The partridge does not ask much of life: a hedgerow under which to shelter from wind and rain, a diet of insects, weed seeds, spilt grain, grasses and leaves, and freedom from predators, particularly at nesting time. Releasing them may take a little more work than releasing pheasants, and they are certainly less easy to manage once they have left their pens, but for the sportsman who relishes the wilder aspect of shooting they will score over pheasants every time.

Grouse

If the partridge is the cream of the lowland game birds, the grouse is the undisputed king of the uplands. Living exclusively on heather moorland, it will either be present on your shoot or it will not. There are no game farms to sell you grouse poults by the thousand, no tried and tested methods of organising a release to boost stocks. If you have heather moorland or hill ground which holds a stock of grouse then you can do a great deal to improve it, but unless you have that moorland to begin with no grouse will feature in your bag on shoot days.

A great deal of research has been, and continues to be, done to try and discover the reasons for the decline of the grouse and ways in which it can be reversed. I understand

Ptarmigan shooting will only be possible if your ground is in the Highlands and runs above the 2,000-foot contour.

French partridges can be released to provide sport over the roughest of hill pasture.

that there are experiments being carried out currently to try and restock moors with grouse brought in from other areas, or to foster artificially produced grouse chicks on barren pairs of adult grouse living in the wild. There are also grants and incentives available for heather regeneration which is probably one of the most important factors in arresting the decline of our most sporting game bird. Ironically, much of the original destruction of our heather moorlands came about as a direct result of government grants and incentives to plant trees or to turn moorland into grazing land by liming the heather and reseeding to produce grass pastures.

If you do have suitable ground for grouse, and an existing stock, then a programme of heather burning, strict vermin control, and the provision of grit, in addition perhaps to a close look at the stocking density of grazing animals, is the accepted way of encouraging that stock to increase. Where the land is suitable there is no finer game bird in the world than the red grouse. If the land is not suitable – that is to say if it is anything other than heather moorland – then nothing will persuade grouse to live there.

Ducks and Geese

It is a little cavalier to lump together the dozen or more species of wildfowl which may be shot in Britain, but in very broad terms what will encourage one species of duck will also encourage another, whereas geese, rather like grouse, are either there or they are not. If you happen to own a farm along certain parts of the Solway, for example, you may well have upwards of 10,000 barnacle geese feeding on your grass during the winter, and 10,000 beaks can quickly make enormous inroads into the grass which you expected to see your sheep through to the spring. The fact that you may no longer shoot barnacles, except under special licence, means that they have no relevance as a sporting species, but the principle is the same for pinks and greylags. If you have got them you may have an overabundance; if you have not got them, then you may as well forget them – unless of course your shoot is in a 'goosey' area, in which case you may be able to decoy them onto your ground.

Duck, on the other hand, can be found practically anywhere apart from the tops of the hills. Rivers, lakes, lochs, ponds, flooded water meadows, drainage ditches, sewage farms, dykes and canals – anywhere where there is enough water for them to dabble will attract them, particularly if you provide a little incentive in the form of a regular supply of food. The feeding of flight ponds for duck is a practice that has increased to an extraordinary extent in recent years, and where once all that was needed was to throw in a little grain every night to pull ducks by the hundred, the range of alternative feeding sites open to them now means that they can be much more selective. Even so, if you have some open water on the shoot in a spot which will not be subject to too much disturbance there is every chance that you can attract enough ducks to provide a regular evening flight.

Mallard can also be reared and released, much like pheasants and partridges, but it may be difficult to provide decent sport with them as they have a tendency to become too tame and may refuse to fly on shoot days. This can be avoided by good management, but it is a factor to beware of if you decide to release some ducks instead of relying on attracting wild birds to the shoot.

Any water at all can hold duck, although the deep, barren-edged lochs of the Highlands offer little attraction for them. The smallest of splashes can pull in a few birds every night

Beaters heading for a larch plantation.

once they discover the food and realise that they will not be disturbed as they eat it. Ideally a flight pond would have shallow margins for dabbling combined with deeper areas to keep the fowl secure from foxes. Weedy margins help to provide cover, both for the ducks and for the guns on flighting evenings, and an island or two where the birds can haul out and preen in safety will be popular. If your shoot does not already have a flight pond it can be quite easy to create one, given a wet corner somewhere, the blessing of the land-owner and a few hours with a JCB. Duck will find it remarkably quickly and could be flighting in almost before the digger has finished work.

Snipe

On many shoots snipe are little more than a bonus, cropping up from time to time in the course of a drive or while walking up. Other shoots may have whole drives – or even whole days – devoted solely to snipe. In some ways, snipe are like grouse, and will only be found in numbers with any degree of certainty where the ground is suitable. However, the odd snipe can appear almost anywhere, from open moorland to a wet splash in the corner of a field; from a wide open estuary to a tiny drainage ditch. Often ignored by the driven shot simply because there is not the time nor the organisation to hunt out the little corners where they may be found, they can be a positive delight to the rough shot, springing suddenly from the most unlikely places and providing a testing target with their twisting, jinking flight.

They favour wet, marshy ground and can congregate in considerable numbers on quite small boggy patches. If you have any rushy fields or water meadows you may be able to organise snipe drives which can provide exciting (and sometimes dangerous) shooting for a team of guns. A snipe flickering low across the rushes in the half-light of evening is a difficult enough target if you are shooting alone. If you also have to consider the position of your neighbouring guns, as well as the beaters or walking guns, then it can be an almost impossible mark – or a positive invitation to fire a dangerous shot.

Hard weather on their favoured feeding grounds can force snipe onto land where they would not normally be found, and a cold snap may push them all down onto the shore away from the frozen ground inland. There is no certainty: the most inviting-looking snipe bog may never hold more than the odd bird, while they can also be flushed from the most unlikely places. Unless you are taking on a marsh or bog shoot specifically for snipe it is probable that you will see them mainly as a welcome addition to the other quarry on your shoot. Where the appropriate conditions exist you can encourage them by spreading dung or blood, which will in turn encourage the worms on which they feed. And of course, it is quite feasible to create a snipe bog by returning formerly boggy ground to the state it was in prior to being ditched and drained – although this may not be popular with farming interests.

Woodcock

The woodcock is another bird that you either have or not – with the added uncertainty that even if you have them today, you may not tomorrow. Some woodcock do stay in Britain to breed in the summer months but the majority of the birds you will find during the shooting season will be migrants from their breeding grounds in Scandinavia, Russia and northern Europe. They arrive during October and November and seem to track slowly across the country from north-east to south-west, leaving a few – or possibly many – of their number behind in woods and copses along the way.

It is easy to generalise about the kind of habitat that woodcock prefer, but far more difficult to be specific. Generally they require woodland in which to shelter during the day, with damp or boggy ground nearby for them to flight out to for feeding at night, but they can also be found in bracken banks and even out on the open hill in broad daylight. Holly and rhododendron bushes will often shelter a bird or two, and rather like salmon lies, a spot that has held one woodcock is likely to attract another. Some woods are a sure magnet for woodcock, season after season, while others may attract a good stock of birds one year – or during one part of the year – and then hold none at all the following season. Other coverts may seem ideal for woodcock but never hold a bird.

They appreciate a quiet life, so woods where they are not disturbed daily by walkers, children playing or even keepers feeding pheasants may prove more attractive than similar coverts which see more human activity. In parts of Ireland, western Scotand and the West Country there are shoots, or beats on shoots, which are run specifically for woodcock, and they can provide superb, wild shooting, but in most cases the woodcock is a welcome addition to the drive or the rough shoot, rather than the main quarry. They can sometimes be found in the most unlikely places, though equally, some of the most likely-looking coverts may never hold a bird, so it is almost impossible to tell on a first inspection whether or not your new shoot will produce a bag of woodcock. Shoot records are a better indica-

Newly planted woodland can be attractive to pheasants for sunning on bright winter days.

tion, and the advice of anyone who has local knowledge, but the best method of all is to get out into the coverts with a good dog any time from October through to January.

Rabbits and Pigeons

The rabbit and the pigeon may seem strange bedfellows, but I shall consider them together because of the things they have in common. Both can be a considerable pest to farmers, but both can also provide first-class sport for the gun. Indeed, all beaters will be familiar with the clap of wings followed by the rattle of musketry that echoes around the woods a few seconds after the beating team first enters a covert. Pigeons are the usual target, and it is quite instructive sometimes to count the shots fired in that first flurry and then look at the number of pigeons accounted for. Indeed, if pigeons could be 'held' in the woods like pheasants and produced for the guns on demand, I suggest that they would rival any of the 'better-class' game birds which some sportsmen will pay so dearly to shoot.

Two major factors will decide whether you can enjoy regular pigeon shooting, or whether you will be restricted to the odd bird which happens along on a shooting day. The first is the type of farming practised on your shoot, and the second is whether your woods are favoured roosting sites for the local pigeon population. If that is the case then you may be able to enjoy some sporting shooting right through the year simply by taking yourself off to the woods as the birds are coming in to roost from their feeding grounds. As far as the type of farming is concerned, cereals, peas, beans, rape, turnips, cabbages, sprouts, clover and a host of other crops will all attract flocks of pigeons – flocks which can cause

considerable damage unless they are checked. If they are a problem the farmers on your shoot will soon let you know, and will quite possibly expect you to help deal with the problem on their behalf.

Rabbits are not, in most cases, anything like the pest that they were before the scourge of that dreadful disease, myxomatosis. I can remember the days when every harvest field was surrounded by a strip, perhaps 20 yards wide, which had been eaten clean by the rabbits, and I can still recall the thousands upon thousands of pathetic dead and dying animals that littered the countryside during the first outbreak. The disease still breaks out quite regularly, but its effects are less widespread, and it seems that more rabbits are either resistant to the virus or able to recover from it.

That said, there are plenty of areas which hold an extremely healthy population of rabbits, and which can form the basis of an excellent rough shoot or provide sport for the ferreter. There is no difficulty in assessing the potential of your shoot for rabbits: all you have to do is walk around and use your eyes. As with pigeons, the farmers on the shoot may be looking to you to control the rabbit population, and a clause to this effect is common in many shooting leases. If you are hoping to enjoy much sport shooting rabbits you should make sure that the control of the population is not already assigned to some other party. Although myxomatosis is no longer the threat to rabbits that it once posed another scourge, viral haemorrhagic disease (VHD), has almost wiped out the rabbit in some parts of the country.

Driven Shoot or Rough Shoot?

You do not necessarily have to choose between rough or driven shooting. Many a rough shoot will include the odd drive when conditions allow it, and there may be bits of ground on even the most formal of driven shoots that are best shot by hunting them out with a good spaniel in the course of an outside day. Indeed, in the case of many of the smaller, do-it-yourself types of shoot it can be a moot point as to whether it is best described as a rough shoot with pretensions or as a driven shoot with down-market tendencies. However, if your inclination veers particularly to one type of shooting or another, you will need to assess the suitability of the ground for that type.

It is far easier to go rough shooting on a driven shoot than it is to adapt a rough shoot for driving. By its very nature rough shooting can take place anywhere there is quarry to be shot. To drive game successfully, however, you really need a shoot layout which will provide points to drive the game to and from, with somewhere to position the guns in between. The classic layout for a driven pheasant shoot will see a number of smallish coverts or plantings of game crop which will encourage the birds to fly in a particular direction when flushed – back to their original release pen, for example, or across to another area of cover. Pheasants can be quite predictable, if they have somewhere to aim themselves at when they fly. If they are simply flushed at random from the middle of the only patch of cover for miles they could take off in any direction at all, and often simply flip around and land back in another part of the same wood.

The rough shoot works best when the game is dispersed all over the shoot. Much of the fun of rough shooting comes from not knowing quite when or where the next shot will be taken; from watching the dogs hunt and trying to outsmart the quarry. Driven shooting relies more on game being held and concentrated in known areas so that beaters and guns can work as a team to fill the game cart. If your ground has a number of small woods and spinneys close enough together for the pheasants, clumsy fliers that they are, to make the distance between them, then you have the basis on which to build your driven shoot. If however, you are taking on a single 1,000-acre block of forestry plantation, or a few hundred acres of mixed woodland, then you may have considerable difficulty in planning and executing your drives to your total satisfaction.

On more open farmland or hills, where partridges may be the quarry, you have a slightly different problem since the partridge is far less predictable in its choice of daytime quarters than the pheasant, and is also a lot less predictable in its flight lines once you have managed to locate it. Whole chapters of shooting books used to be devoted to the military-style manoeuvres employed to put partridges over a line of guns. In practice, there is no substitute for experience. And if this is the case with the partridge it is even more so with grouse. A single grouse drive can take in thousands of acres of moorland, and may well begin with the beaters half a mile or more away from the butts, and quite possibly heading in the opposite direction.

It is hard to imagine any type of ground that would not be suitable for rough shooting. A rough shoot can be organised practically anywhere where there is game and enough room to walk after it. Driven shooting, and particularly driven pheasant shooting, requires a slightly more specialised layout. You *can* organise drives on almost any ground, but your task will be greatly simplified if there is a pattern of cover, be it woodland, scrub, agricultural crops or game crop, which offers the birds in one patch of cover an easy and obvious place to fly to when flushed. There is a great deal that can be done to improve things if the natural cover pattern is inadequate, but only if the ground lends itself to such improvements and the terms of the lease will permit them. If your shoot is totally devoted to mature forestry, for example, or if it lacks the right pattern of cover and the growing of game crop is not permitted, then it may be difficult, though not necessarily impossible, to produce driven pheasants with any consistency.

Wild Birds or Released Stock?

This is another of those questions that may be answered for you, particularly in the first year or so of the shoot. If you are starting from scratch, and there is little or no game on the shoot, you may have no choice but to release some birds if you are to enjoy any shooting at all in the first year. On the other hand, you may be a little more fortunate in your chosen ground and be starting off with a stock of pheasants or partridges already in place – perhaps both if you are really lucky. In that case the choice may be between releasing more birds or relying on the existing stock to breed well enough to sustain the shoot.

At first sight the obvious conclusion might be to do both: to encourage the wild stock to multiply while boosting their numbers with released birds. This may well be a viable option, although there are one or two possible pitfalls for the shoot manager who seeks to hedge his bets in this manner. The first is that in trying to cope with the released birds insufficient attention may be paid to vermin control, particularly the control of crows and foxes in the spring and early summer. If you have too many predators taking a toll of your wild stock then very few young birds will survive to maturity. The farming pattern can also have a devastating effect on the wild stock. Cutting fields for silage in the middle of the nesting season, or spraying crops prior to hatching time and destroying the insects that chicks rely on for food can effectively wipe out your replacement stock. There is also some evidence that released partridges, in competing for territory with the wild birds already on the ground, may positively harm their prospects of breeding and regenerating your stock naturally.

The problem for the part-time or do-it-yourself keeper is also likely to be that he simply does not have sufficient time to cope with all the work that needs to be done at the same time. With the laying pen, the rearing field and the release pen being the more immediate and obvious priorities it is the reared birds that tend to receive the attention, while the wild stock is left to cope as best it can.

Running a shoot entirely on wild game is an attractive idea, and where it can be achieved it can provide excellent shooting, but it is not the low-cost option that it might seem at first. The time that is needed to keep the shoot clear of egg, chick and adult bird predators, and to manage the habitat to suit the breeding birds, may prove more costly than buying in poults and building a release pen. The other major point in favour of releasing game is that the shoot manager has much greater control over the numbers of birds present when shooting starts. There is, of course, no guarantee of success with either released birds or wild game. The game farm, however, is much less at the mercy of the

Pheasants will breed in the wild, but only if their predators are kept under control.

weather, of predators and of all the other chance elements that can adversely effect wild stock. That said, there are certain diseases which may cause havoc among the intensively stocked birds of a rearing unit, and even such a simple thing as a power cut can wipe out months of work.

If you are looking to enjoy a few days' rough shooting, and will be content with whatever bag you are lucky enough to find on the day, then leaving things to nature may be your best and most cost-effective option. If, however, you want to organise eight or ten driven days, with the bag averaging a particular figure, then it is probable that you will plan to release at least some of your birds. And of course, if your quarry is grouse, woodcock, snipe, rabbits or pigeons, then the question of releasing game will never arise.

It is possible, by dint of a great deal of hard work, to introduce pheasants to ground which may not particularly suit them, and to hold them there through the shooting season. It is considerably harder to do the same thing with partridges, although again it is not impossible. Other, wilder species such as grouse, snipe and woodcock will decide themselves where they live, and though you may do a number of things to encourage them to visit your shoot, if the ground is not suitable they will simply not be there. In every case, however, you are more likely to succeed if you can work with nature rather than against it. It is far better to assess the potential of the ground with an open mind, and then to

Good dogs, like this springer spaniel, are essential to find and flush birds where cover is dense.

work to encourage the game that will occur there by its own choice than it is to attempt to force birds to live in a habitat that does not suit them. You can, of course, take steps to create suitable habitat, but you are more likely to succeed in, for example, holding a stock of partridges on rough, open hill grazing where they may live quite naturally, than in persuading pheasants to stay there by spending a great deal of money on creating game cover crops or small woodlands which may still not hold them.

You can create a flight pond almost anywhere, provided you are prepared to dig it out, line the hole with plastic and pump enough water in to fill it, but you will find the task far simpler if you site it in a wet hollow where the rain and the run-off from the fields will fill it naturally. Besides, the ducks are more likely to be attracted to a natural-looking pond than to an obviously artificial one.

In short, you should look to develop your shoot by encouraging the best of the natural advantages, whatever they are, rather than by trying to impose an alien culture on the ground. Such a philosophy is likely to prove more effective in the long term at providing the best and most sporting shooting that your ground can offer, and in the short term it will probably be cheaper to implement. There will also be less likelihood of making costly errors which will stay to haunt you for years to come. And of course, if the natural way does not work as you would wish you can always turn to alternative methods in future years.

5 Releasing Pheasants and Partridges

Ideally, there should be no need to release game, either pheasants or partridges, in order to provide shooting. In a perfect world a shoot would hold a natural stock of wild game which would breed in the spring and raise sufficient young during the summer months to allow us to crop the surplus population during the autumn and winter – taking care, of course, to leave sufficient stock on the ground to provide the next year's shootable surplus.

There are still plenty of shoots which do operate along these lines, and if you are fortunate enough to obtain such a treasure you should enjoy it to the full, and appreciate just how· lucky you are to have it. It is likely, however, that the prime factor in creating such a shoot is not luck, but is a lot – an awful lot – of hard work. You can run a shoot solely on wild game, and it can provide more than just the odd, token bird on shoot days, but there are several factors which will have to be in place before it will happen.

First, the habitat must be suitable to hold pheasants, partridges or grouse, and it must be suitable to hold them *right through the year*. It is one thing to release pheasants and keep them on the shoot through the autumn and winter with the aid of regular feeding and the natural cover that slowly dies back through the winter, but it is quite another to provide them with suitable nesting cover through spring and early summer, plus the natural food that the chicks will require when they are hatched. You can hold 1,000 pheasant poults in a single release pen prior to the shooting season, but you can hardly expect 100 wild pheasant hens to settle down to nest in that same pen in the spring. If you have 100 nesting hens, then you must have 100 suitable nesting sites spread across the shoot – and some hen pheasants are notoriously bad at selecting nesting sites. The farming methods must be sympathetic to the needs of ground-nesting birds, and lend themselves to providing cover and food for chicks, and there must be somewhere for the birds to make their home when the crops are harvested.

Secondly, you must have sufficient stock on the ground to provide a shootable surplus, or you must be prepared to forgo, or strictly limit, your shooting for a season, or several seasons, until the stock has had a chance to build up. This is not just a matter of not shooting for a year or two. If the ground only holds the odd pheasant when you take it over it is possible that this is because the ground – which means both the geography of the land and the way in which it is used for farming or forestry – is only suitable for the odd wild bird. If so, you may have a great deal of work to do before there is any possibility of a wild bird shoot beginning to take off.

Thirdly, there must be tight control of predators, particularly of foxes and corvids during the spring nesting period. There is no point whatsoever in having a healthy stock of game birds spending weeks in the spring laying and incubating eggs, if those eggs and chicks are simply going to provide a source of protein for fox cubs and crows. Foxes will take sitting hens, eggs and chicks, although the fox is possibly less destructive to game birds than members of the crow family, particularly carrion crows, hooded crows and magpies. They will hunt the ground systematically for nesting birds, and then plunder eggs and chicks alike. If there are too many crows on the ground then few if any pheasants or partridges will rear a brood to maturity – and it does not take many crows to qualify as 'too many'.

The logical alternative to enjoying a wild bird shoot is to release artificially reared birds onto the shoot. Although the work involved in building release pens, feeding and watering the poults in the pen and the released birds in the fields or coverts, and generally managing the birds through the shooting season, is considerable, it is also more easily quantifiable than the somewhat nebulous tasks involved in running a wild bird shoot. It is not necessarily an easy alternative. Looking after pheasant or partridge poults can involve a great deal of hard work. However, it is possible to plan out the work and costs involved in running a release programme with much more certainty than doing the same exercise for a wild bird shoot.

You can decide on the day when the poults will be delivered – subject to the vagaries of the weather and the schedule of the game farm. You can choose to feed your birds daily by scattering wheat onto straw rides, or weekly – perhaps even fortnightly – by using hoppers. You can decide whether to have all the poults in a single release pen or whether to have half a dozen separate pens scattered around the shoot. In the case of partridges it may be twenty, thirty, perhaps even fifty pens, distributed around the shoot, but we will deal with that matter later. You can decide whether you will start off with 100 poults or with 10,000, and thus whether you will be shifting 1 ton of wheat during the season or 100 tons. In short, you will have much more control over the shoot, much more influence over the number of birds and the number of days' shooting you can enjoy and much more control over costs. You will not, however, have the hunter's satisfaction of shooting truly wild birds. On balance, most newly established shoots will have to release birds if they are to enjoy any sort of consistent shooting season by season, as indeed do the majority of long-established shoots.

Release Pens

A release pen serves three main purposes, whether it is designed for pheasants or for partridges. First, it concentrates the birds in an area of your choice when they are first released, and keeps them there until they have become hefted to the area. Without a pen of some kind it is likely that the majority of released poults would wander and die, or be killed, within a day or two of being released. Equally importantly, it protects the poults from predators, particularly foxes, cats, dogs, badgers, mink and the like during the period when they are most vulnerable, immediately after release. Finally, it provides a 'home base' for the birds long after they have spread out across the rest of the shoot. In the case of pheasants the pen is often the place to which the birds will fly when they are flushed from a covert or game crop during a drive, with partridges the pen may provide a natural and, depending on the design, predator-resistant site for roosting at night and resting during the day.

Plastic drum mounted on posts to form a water reservoir.

Although the pen serves the same main purpose whether the birds released are pheasants or partridges, the management of the birds differs radically. However, the main objective is the same in both cases: to settle the birds down to life in the wild while minimising losses due to predation, bad weather or simply wandering off the shoot. Once this has been achieved the aim is to manage the birds in such a way that they will provide difficult and sporting shooting, with a sufficient proportion brought to bag to justify the time and expense of the release programme.

I do not propose to speculate on what is an acceptable percentage return, since this will vary considerably from shoot to shoot. As an example, I help to run a driven pheasant shoot where experience has shown that we normally shoot around 45 per cent of the birds we release. We consider that to be a perfectly satisfactory return, given the nature of the ground, the level of stocking on neighbouring shoots and the particular problems of showing game over the guns on our shoot. In a very good year we have achieved a 60 per cent return, but that was aided by a particularly good summer and an exceptionally tractable batch of poults. But I am also a partner in a high-ground shoot, where we release a few partridges in order to shoot over our pointers and setters. In the first few years of running the shoot our returns have averaged below 20 per cent; indeed in one year we failed to make even 10 per cent – but as far as I and my partners were concerned the shoot was a success. We spent a number of highly enjoyable days working the dogs out on the hill; we shot a few birds on some of those days and on others they were too good for us. Overall, however, the sport we enjoyed was well worth the money and effort we invested, so the shoot was, by my definition, a success. Percentage returns are interesting to compare year with year, or even shoot with shoot, but there is no magic figure at which a shoot may be declared a success or a failure. Only you can be the judge of that.

It is possible to release poults successfully without using a pen – and by 'successfully' I mean that the birds will remain alive and on the shoot after the release. However, unless you have mounted an extremely rigorous campaign against the predators on the shoot, and unless the shoot itself is particularly inviting to the newly released poults, it is an extremely risky business. You will save the expense of building a pen, but you do so at the very real risk of losing most, if not all, of the birds you release. And while a pen might be an expensive investment in the first year, it will, if properly constructed, serve for many years to come.

Whether you plan to release pheasants or partridges, and whether your release programme is going to cater for 100 birds or for 10,000, there are a number of factors that must be considered. We will look at the individual requirements of pheasants and partridges shortly, and the features that must be included if there is to be any real chance of a successful release programme, but to begin, let us consider those matters which all release pens have in common.

Access

It may seem obvious, but you have to be able to get to the pen, and get there in all weathers. There is the initial problem of carting wire netting, fence posts, feeders and drinkers, electric fencing units, batteries, gates, tin sheets for shelters and all the tools you will need to build the pen in the first instance, and then there is the matter of getting food, and possibly water, out to supply the poults while they are in the pen. You may be able to drive a

Two patent drinkers which are fed from the plastic reservoir drum.

truck across the stubbles to the edge of the wood with no trouble at all in the warmth of a September evening, but how will you get there in November when the stubble has been turned into a sea of soft, sticky ploughed mud? How will you get there before the crops have been harvested if your only access is by driving across the fields?

The ideal site for your pen from the shooting point of view may be in the middle of a 100-acre wood, halfway up a steep hillside. You may be able to raise enough helpers to make light work of carrying the materials for the pen, but how will you manage when you have to carry food and water in to the poults every day? If you only have 100 young pheasants to cater for, eating perhaps 15–20 pounds of wheat or pellets each day, then there may be no problem at all for you to trot up the hill with half a bag of food on your back each morning. But what if you have put 1,000 birds in that pen, and they are going to require the better part of 2 hundredweight of wheat daily, not to mention 10 gallons of water? Will you be able to carry that lot up the hill and through the trees? Of course, you could cut a ride through the wood, buy an all-terrain vehicle and drive up there like a gentleman – provided that the shoot budget would stand the cost. Or you could site the pen somewhere that you can reach easily and spend the money on an extra 1,000 poults.

A site that is easily accessible for one shoot might be totally out of bounds to another. When considering access you must also consider the vehicles available to you, and your relationship with the farmer or farming tenant. If he is a member of the shoot he may be quite willing to leave you a track along a headland to allow you to drive across the fields to the pen. If not you might have your ears bent the first time he spots a sign of a wheel track on one of his fields. Even if you are allowed to drive over the fields, do you have a vehicle that will cope with the conditions when the ground is wet and muddy?

There may be no problems of access at all, but it is essential that you try to anticipate any that might crop up before you start driving in stakes and hanging netting. It is no good suddenly finding yourself with a pen full of poults and no way to feed them apart from carting sacks of wheat on your back over ½ mile of heavy, ploughed clay. There are more enjoyable ways to keep fit.

Public Access

It is an unpleasant fact that shooting is becoming more and more a target for anti-field-sports activists. A pen full of poults makes an easy target, and the fact that 'liberating' them by tearing down the fences is likely to be a death sentence for most of them will not stop some idealistic idiot from doing just that. If you site your release pen close to a road or track which is used by the public then you must at least consider the danger of having your work destroyed by a gang of louts who neither understand nor care about the countryside and country matters. That we should even need to consider such matters when pursuing a legal and traditional country sport is a sad reflection on society today, but it is nevertheless an important consideration for every shoot manager. Much will depend on where your shoot is situated, and on the attitude of the local police, who may or may not be willing to get involved in protecting your property and prosecuting those who would damage it. This type of attack may not be common in your area, but it is worth remembering that the protesters are becoming increasingly mobile. Siting a pen in a place where it will draw attention to itself is adding one extra danger to those already faced by poults starting to make their way in the wild.

It is not only the committed anti-field-sports activists who may prove a thorn in your side if your pen is too easily accessible to the public. If it is close to a busy road you are almost certain to lose a number of birds to passing traffic. Pheasants are not noted for their road sense nor, sadly, are many drivers. Far too many pious souls who would condemn you outright as a cruel sadist because you choose to shoot pheasants will think nothing of deliberately mowing them down with their cars.

You must also consider the effect that dog-walkers and the like may have on your poults, not to mention the sort of mischief that children can create simply by leaving gates open or putting the poults to flight at roosting time. They may not mean to create havoc, but a gate left open, allowing a fox to gain entry, is just as devastating whether it is done maliciously or not. In short, while access is vital for you, you must balance the ease with which you can reach the pen with the possible danger to your birds if the public also enjoy that right.

Finally, if your pen is too easily reached, you may find your poults targeted by poachers. This can be a problem wherever you site the pen, but there is a great deal to be said for not dangling temptation in front of a poacher. Ideally, your pen should be far enough from the public gaze to allow your poults to mature in peace, while still being simple enough of access to allow you to reach it whenever you need to and whatever the weather.

Shoot Strategy

A release pen is not just a means to getting birds onto the shoot. In siting the pen you will also be determining a great deal of the birds' future behaviour. The pen will be their home for several weeks, perhaps months, and may well be the place where they will return to roost at night, and to which they will fly for shelter when they are flushed during the day. A classic pheasant shoot would have a release pen centrally sited with coverts radiating out from it. Once the birds had begun to leave the pen they would be encouraged to move into the outlying woods, the intention on shoot days being to drive them back towards the pen where they would – or should – be most willing to fly. It follows therefore, that you should be looking further ahead than just releasing the birds when you consider the site of your pen or pens.

The ideal site for a pen where the aim is to provide driven shooting might be completely different from the best site if you wanted to establish a rough shoot on the same ground. In any event, the choice of site will almost certainly represent a compromise. The wood which is easiest of access may also be too near to a public road or path. The best wood for poults in terms of cover, roosting trees and sunning glades may also be situated right on the boundary of the shoot and thus represent an open invitation for your birds to wander off the ground. The best-located covert may be too thick, too thin, too cold or too difficult to reach. There may not be any choice at all, in that there may be only one wood in which you are able to site your pen. Ideally, however, if you do have a choice, you should look beyond the immediate needs of your poults, important though these are, and consider the overall plan for the shoot when deciding on the site or sites.

Pheasants

A seven-week-old pheasant poult which has grown up in a rearing pen can have little idea of what life in the real world will be like. Wild pheasant chicks have the advantage of following their mother around from the day they are hatched and learning by example the need to hide from predators, to be inconspicuous as they move around and to forage for seeds and insects to fill their crops. Contrast this with a reared poult which is suddenly uplifted from the covered run and heated brooder house which has been its home since hatching and is turfed out into the wild along with a few hundred of its equally naive fellows. They have seven weeks of learning to catch up on, and they need to do it as quickly as possible. Slow learners will simply not live long enough to absorb the necessary knowledge.

The pen needs to provide them with a microcosm of the world they will find once they start to move out onto the main part of the shoot. They need some thick undergrowth – brambles, nettles, bracken, rhododendrons, rushes, scrubby bushes or long grass – in which they can hide from predators and seek shelter from the wind and rain. They need some clear, sunny areas where they can dry their feathers after rain and scratch about in the warmth of the sunny days which you hope they will get immediately after their release. They need trees to roost in, so that the habit of sleeping off the ground and out of reach of four-legged predators is established before they move out from the relative safety of the pen. They need something to keep them occupied so that they will not start wandering off before they are streetwise enough to cope with life beyond the wire. When you choose the

A simple feeder made by hanging a plastic drum from a tree.

sites for your release pens you must bear all this in mind, and try to match as many of the criteria as possible.

If there is a lack of open spaces you may be able to make some with a little judicious application of a chain-saw, possibly creating a little extra ground cover at the same time by leaving the brashings and branches piled up on the floor of the pen. You can plant shrubs and bushes to provide cover, and build shelters by roofing four short posts with corrugated iron sheets. Poults will not only shelter from the rain under these, but they will also sit on top of them to catch the breeze and the sun, while the dry soil underneath a shelter provides the ideal site for birds taking dust baths.

Once you have selected your site you can get on with the business of building the pen. We have just erected a new pen using chain-link fencing which was bought for next to nothing from a motorway construction firm which was clearing a site, but the normal material for the fence would be small-mesh wire netting. The walls need to be around 6 feet high, and the netting should be turned out for 1 foot or so at the base to prevent predators burrowing underneath. It is also useful to have 1 foot or so left to flop outwards at the top to discourage anything that might try and climb in, so you actually need a height of about 8 feet of netting. Some shoots use plastic netting for the top half of the run, or wider-meshed wire netting, but it is important that the lower 3 feet or so of the fence is made with a mesh narrow enough to stop the poults pushing their heads through, and to prevent small predators such as stoats and weasels from squeezing in.

Posts can consist of whatever you can lay your hands on. It is cheapest to cut your own, but they are likely to rot in fairly short order. Proper fence posts which have been pressure treated are supposed to last for twenty years, but they are also quite expensive. Angle iron will rust eventually, but if you can get hold of iron posts – perhaps from someone who is ripping down an old fence – they should last at least as long as wooden stakes.

You need to select a clear pathway to run the fence along, or to cut a ride all round the perimeter. There is no point erecting a fence to keep predators out if they can simply shin up a tree and then drop into the pen, nor is it ideal to encourage your poults to roost in the trees if they will be able to drop down outside the fence in the mornings. You may well not be permitted to fell much, if any, standing timber in order to clear the run of your fence, but if you are able to provide a 3-yard corridor round the pen it will be well worth the extra work involved in cutting it.

There used to be a rule of thumb regarding the size of release pens which said that there should be a yard of perimeter fence for every bird in the pen. However, let us contrast two pens, one a square with four sides each 50 yards long, and one a rectangle 80 yards long and 20 yards wide. Both have a perimeter of 200 yards, but the square pen covers almost 40 per cent more area. I would suggest that you make the pen as large as your covert and your pocket will allow. Your birds will certainly not suffer because the pen is too

A 'peck' feeder with legs and a metal disc which will release a few grains of wheat when the pheasants peck at it.

large, whereas too small a pen will encourage feather-pecking and disease as well as quickly becoming defoliated and muddy. Besides, you may well want to increase the number of birds that you release, and an over-sized pen will allow you to do this without any extra construction work.

It helps if there are no sharp corners in which the birds can become piled up if they should panic at a passing buzzard or something of that kind. Corners also help to trap birds and make them liable to pegging by beaters' dogs if the pen is to be used as part of one of your drives. And the gate or gates must be at least as secure as the rest of the pen because if there is a weak spot you can guarantee that a predator will find it. A hungry fox, badger or cat will devote a lot of time to probing your defences and any chinks will be found and exploited.

Your poults, in the early stages at least, will almost certainly show considerable ingenuity in fluttering, flying and flapping out over the wire, whether you have wing-clipped them or not. It is equally certain that once outside, nothing will persuade them to fly back in. They will, however, march round and round the perimeter fence, peeping away to their friends inside the wire. In order to get them back where they belong pop-holes should be built at regular intervals along the fence. These are simply gaps in the fence, protected with a fox-proof grid, and with 'wings' of netting set out at an angle from the fence to guide the birds back into the pen. Inside the pen is a tunnel of netting which narrows near the inside. This tunnel allows the outside birds to squeeze back in, but prevents all but the most dedicated escapees from getting out.

A metal grid with a gap of between 3½ and 4 inches will allow a poult to squeeze in while preventing a fox from doing the same thing. Some keepers, principally those who wing-clip their birds, advocate blocking off these grids until the birds start to find their way out of the pen, in case fox cubs or other small predators use them to get in, but it has been my experience that some poults will find a way out almost from the moment they are put into the pen. If you are desperately trying to shepherd forty or fifty little bodies back where they belong on the evening of the day they were released, you will not welcome the extra task of extracting a netting bung from each pop-hole before you can start to ease them back in again.

The birds will naturally be stressed at suddenly finding themselves in strange surroundings and may be reluctant to eat or drink properly for the first day or two. You can help to prevent this by putting out plenty of drinkers, perhaps just in the form of flat trays of water, plus a number of egg trays or something similar with extra feed on them. It does not require much – just a handful or so on each egg tray, but it does help to get some sustenance into the poults in the first couple of days in the open. Scatter these about all over the pen and particularly round the perimeter fence, and they will help the chicks to feed and drink in the first few days until they get used to the regular feeders and drinkers. It may waste a little food, particularly if there is rain, but it may also save a few poults and give the majority of them a slightly better start to life in the pen.

Once the birds settle down they will start to become bored with their surroundings and may tend to wander off, or become prone to vices such as feather-pecking. You can help curb this by giving them something to keep them occupied: straw rides with wheat scattered thinly through the straw, a few rabbits hung up so that they will become fly-blown and thus drop maggots onto the ground for them to eat, some waste vegetables tossed about for them to peck at, perhaps a few straw bales laid out here and there for them to scratch at and clamber over – in fact anything that keeps them amused will help to keep them at home and out of mischief.

Once they do start to leave the shelter of the pen you may find that it is necessary to 'dog them in', particularly in the evenings, to prevent them from wandering off the shoot. This can be excellent experience for steadying a young gundog, but it can also be extremely time-consuming, especially when you have more than enough other work to keep you busy on the shoot already. Nevertheless, if you can spend a little time edging the poults back towards the pen at this stage it may be justified by a considerable rise in the bag later in the year.

The defences of most release pens are supplemented by one or two strands of electrified fence wire strung around the perimeter. These should be placed at about 6 inches and 1 foot from the ground, the intention being that any passing fox, cat, dog or badger will receive a sharp sting on the nose and thus lose interest in the pen before discovering what an easy source of free protein it can provide. You must make sure that the fence is not shorted out by any blades of grass, leaves, twigs or wires from the fence or the battery will quickly became flat and it will lose all its effectiveness. It may help to spray weed killer along the edge of the pen under the electric fence line: otherwise you will have to cut or trim the vegetation before erecting the fence, and quite possibly repeat the treatment at least once during the season.

Once the birds are well established, have got used to roosting in the trees and are mature enough to avoid the attentions of ground predators, it is time to start easing them away

Picking up near the release pen after a drive.

from the release pen and out into the coverts. Keepers who hand-feed daily often use a horn or whistle to call the birds to the rides at feeding time. Once the birds are used to responding to the whistle it can be used to draw them out from the pen and into the coverts, where new feed rides will have been prepared in readiness. If you are hopper feeding it is slightly more difficult, but the birds can be guided in the right direction by gradually moving the hoppers out of the pen and towards the coverts. At the same time you should have full hoppers in position in the coverts so that those birds which go exploring will find them and become familiar with them as providers of food.

When the birds are feeding confidently on the outside feed rides you can stop feeding in the pen itself. This may take a certain amount of courage, especially if you have a lot of birds still using the feeders in the pen. On some shoots, where the pen is also used as a drive, it may be better to keep feeding in the pen right through the season, although many shoots prefer to use the pen as a sort of sanctuary, driving birds *to* it but never *from* it. This aspect of management will obviously vary with every individual shoot and according to the practicalities of planning drives and showing birds over the guns.

Provided it is big enough, a pheasant pen can hold as many birds as you want to put in it. Hundreds, and in some cases even thousands, of birds can be released in a single pen, although if you are planning to release birds by the thousand you will almost certainly be better with a number of smaller pens rather than a single, giant one. It is in this respect that the management of pheasants most differs from that of partridges.

Partridges

Back in the days when the partridge ruled unchallenged as the cream of our low-ground shooting the majority of the partridges killed every autumn – and there were a great many of them – were wild birds. True, they received a lot of help and encouragement in finding nesting sites, hatching their clutches and raising their broods, but in essence the coveys that drew thousands of sportsmen out into the fields from 1 September onwards were there because of the skill of the parent partridges rather than the efforts of the game farmer.

In many cases the accuracy of the term 'wild birds' might be considered to have been severely stretched. One system much in use saw the keepers attempting to locate every partridge nest on the estate in order that they could remove the eggs from under the sitting hen and replace them with wooden, dummy eggs. The real eggs were then hatched in an incubator, or under broody hens, and returned to the rightful mothers just as they were about to hatch. In this way, while the sitting hen was still at risk from predators, her eggs were not. If a hen was taken by a fox or killed by a mowing machine her clutch would be spread around among those that had survived. It was an extremely labour intensive system, and relied heavily on the fact that, once the eggs were returned to the hen and she had completed the process of hatching, the habitat would be suitable for her to raise the brood successfully.

Partridge chicks need a high protein diet, especially in the first two weeks of their lives, and in the wild that protein is derived almost exclusively from insects. Modern farming methods using sprays which destroy insect life almost destroyed the partridge as well – albeit inadvertently – and changed the face of shooting in Britain in the process. There are moves now among many sporting farmers to attempt to redress this matter, and we

Partridges are somewhat wilder than pheasant poults and require slightly different rearing techniques.

will see later how sympathetic farming practices can do much to aid the wild partridge in making a recovery. For the moment though, we are concerned with the releasing of artificially reared partridges onto the shoot, and the ways in which releasing partridges differs from the well-established practice of releasing pheasants.

The partridge is a very family-minded bird and lives, by choice, in a covey or family group. In nature the covey consists of the parent birds, which had paired off to nest in spring, plus their brood – anything up to fifteen or so chicks. They will stay together right through the autumn and winter, forming up again as soon as possible when they are scattered by predators or by the beaters on shooting days. Laudable though this adherence to family values may be, it is also a problem for the shoot manager who wishes to augment the population on his shoot by rearing and releasing a few extra birds.

The problem is that the partridge is quite prepared to consider itself as a member of a much-extended family. If you put 100 partridges into a release pen you will create a 100-strong covey; and while a covey of that size may present a stirring sight on a shooting day, it will not provide very much shooting if the lot fly across the line *en masse*. It will provide even less sport if the whole covey sneaks out on the flank and misses the guns altogether. Coveys of that size do not happen in nature because the wild covey would normally consist simply of parents and their brood, and even if two hens lay in the same nest, as can happen, it is unlikely that a covey would exceed twenty or so birds in total. Five coveys of twenty birds, or ten coveys of ten will provide much better sport for the guns, whether they are walking up, shooting over dogs or driving the birds, than a single, huge flush of 100 partridges, however spectacular it might look.

The answer to the problem is to ensure that you do not create a 'super-covey' in the first place, by releasing your birds in small 'family' groups, through a number of small release pens instead of one large one, and trying to persuade them to settle down in coveys scattered about the shoot.

In fact, even if you wanted to release partridges using a pheasant-sized release pen, you would be unable to do so. A seven-week-old pheasant poult can be quite lively, but beside a partridge poult of the same age it looks almost comatose. Stand a crate of pheasant poults down in the release pen, open the door and step back out of sight, and there is a good chance that they will amble quietly out and conceal themselves under the nearest available cover. Do the same with a crate full of partridge poults and they will come out like the Red Arrows performing a bomb-burst.

So you have to release your partridges in small, covey-sized groups – anything from twenty to fifty birds (though commercial shoots deal in much larger numbers) – and you have to release them into pens which have roof netting as well as side netting. And since you are going to be releasing your birds in small groups you are going to need a number of small pens instead of one or two large ones. The main difference between releasing partridges and pheasants is that, instead of starting with all your birds in one place and then encouraging them to scatter out across the shoot, you will be trying to establish each covey – or each pen of birds – more or less in the area where you hope they will stay.

Whereas a pheasant pen is generally erected in the hope that it will continue to be in use for the next ten years or so, a partridge pen is more likely to be a portable structure, erected for one season only, and quite possibly relocated each year. The easiest way to ensure such portability is to build the pen from prefabricated sections which can be tacked together quickly and easily, and just as easily taken down and relocated when required. The actual size of a section can be varied to suit the timber you have available, and the ease with which you can transport the finished section. We use sections 8 feet long by 4 feet high and build our pens from eight such sections. This gives a pen 16 feet square, which is ample to accommodate thirty or so poults. A smaller pen – perhaps 10 feet square – would be adequate for twenty poults, provided that you started your release programme fairly smartly – but more of that in a moment.

The sections should have a solid plank or two, 6–12 inches high, running along the lower edge. This will give the birds some shelter from the wind and rain, as well as making it a little harder for small predators to squeeze into the pen. The rest of the section should be netted with small-mesh rabbit netting so that the partridges cannot stick their heads through the holes. You need a door in one of the sections, and a net over the top. This should be fine meshed and soft – not wire netting – because the poults will fly up and crash into the top netting with considerable force every time something frightens them – and it does not take very much to frighten a partridge poult. If there are any holes in the net they will either fly out through them or become tangled up and hang themselves. Money spent on good top netting will not be wasted.

Inside the pen you will have to provide at least one feeder, one drinker and something to shelter the poults from the rain. A sheet of corrugated iron fixed to four short posts will suffice for the shelter, or just a triangle of plywood fixed across one corner at the level of the bottom boards. It does not have to be particularly big because thirty partridge poults will huddle together in a surprisingly small space if it is raining hard enough. If you add a straw bale for the birds to climb on and scratch at, you will have provided pretty much everything your poults will require inside the pen.

The next step is to duplicate everything you have put in the pen on the outside. Provide a feeder and a drinker, a tin-roofed shelter, and a straw bale as well if you put one inside. 'Outside' means close to the pen, not two or three fields away as is the case with pheasants, when you are trying to get them to spread out over the shoot. The outside partridge feeders, drinkers and shelters are intended to serve exactly the opposite purpose.

As we have established, a partridge pen should be completely escape-proof, with wood and wire netting sections for sides and a netting roof. Once the poults are put in the pen, leave them to settle down for a week or so, and then allow three or four to get out. In theory you get them to walk out quietly and calmly; in practice they may well leave in full flight and show every sign of flying on until they reach the next county. Once three or four birds have departed, secure the pen again and leave. With any luck the birds you have released will quickly return to their covey, encouraged by the calling of their erstwhile companions. A few days later you should let another four or five go, and keep repeating this until most of the birds are outside and just three or four are kept in.

You will see now why I suggested you should duplicate the feeders, drinkers, shelter and straw bale on the outside, close by the pen. The birds which have been let out need to feel that they are still part of the original covey. By providing them with all their home comforts in close proximity to their captive relations you help to foster that bond. You will often find the two lots of poults sitting close against the wire, one inside and the other outside, in order to maintain contact with each other. And if your release works properly, you will eventually be able to let the whole covey loose with every confidence that they will continue to make their home around the original pen area.

If you plan to release partridges in any numbers then clearly you will require quite a lot of pens. Three or four pens would suffice for 100 poults, and 100 poults can provide you with quite a lot of sport, particularly if they are intended just to add a little bit of variety to a rough shooting day, or to pop up occasionally during a pheasant drive and surprise the guns. If, however, you want to shoot four or five driven partridge days, perhaps shooting 100 birds per day on average, then you are going to have to release considerably more – perhaps 1,000 – and that will mean erecting and servicing a lot of pens.

Partridges are less predictable than pheasants, and considerably harder to persuade to fly in exactly the right direction when the beaters flush them, but this should not be seen as a negative factor. Part of the charm of partridge shooting is precisely that the birds are wilder and less cooperative than pheasants, and making a bag of partridges can require skilled team work between beaters, flankers and guns. You start off with something of an advantage in that you decide where the pens go, and therefore where the partridges will hopefully be found – within reason – when shooting days come around.

It is important to select your pen sites with proper forethought. One consideration, and probably the major one, is that you want the birds to be in roughly the right place on shooting days. If you put the pens too close together there is a danger that the poults will combine into a single large covey, although it is also said that you should not separate the pens too widely so that the individual coveys do not feel totally isolated. You must make up your own mind which theory you will follow. We released four pens of partridges on our hill shoot, with the pens roughly at the corners of a mile-wide square, and two of the coveys still managed to join up from time to time. That said, they also tended to separate back into their original coveys, so it was not a problem. And when you come to site your pens, you are likely to be constrained by the geography of your shoot.

You must obviously select sites where a covey of partridges might reasonably be

Once your poults have been released they may need dogging in to prevent them straying off the shoot.

expected to take up residence, but you must also bear in mind the requirements of a shooting day. Add to that the need to visit every pen on a regular basis, and to be able to reach the pens even after the weather has broken and the fields are wet or ploughed up, and you will see that there is more to siting a partridge pen than simply setting half a dozen sections down in one corner of a stubble field.

Guns gathering after a successful drive.

One of the shoots across the valley from my home released a few pens of partridges for the first time last year. The shoot runs up onto some hill grazing, and the hill is split by three or four deep, steep-sided, bracken-covered gullies. They sited their pens along the tops of the gullies, and produced some spectacular shooting by flushing the birds across them while the guns were standing in line in the gully floors. The partridge were very unpredictable, both in where they would be found and in the direction they were liable to fly when flushed, but on most days enough would fly over the guns to elicit a very satisfying rattle of musketry, although it should also be said that not many featured in the bag at the end of the day. The gullies are very deep, and the partridges provided some very sporting shooting.

If you are planning to release a considerable number of partridges you might consider splitting your pens into two. Start off with both sides full of birds, then release your poults in phases until one side is empty. Then you can introduce more poults into this side while continuing to release the older birds from the other. Once all the older birds are gone you can give the younger ones full access to both sides of the pen, and continue to release them to join the others on the outside of the wire. It is not a system I have tried myself, mainly because we tend to release only a small number of partridges, but also because I shy away from anything that smacks of complication when dealing with game bird poults. There are enough problems caused by the birds themselves without inviting extra ones through your system of management. That said, many shoots do use the split-pen system, and it can certainly save capital outlay on pens, feeders and drinkers while allowing a greater number of birds to be released from the same number of pens.

The actual releasing of the birds can be as simple or as complicated as you choose to make it. I have seen some very elaborate arrangements made with trapdoors controlled by lengths of string let into the sides of the pens, the idea being that you can open up the door, let three or four birds out, and then close it again, all from a safe distance to avoid frightening the birds as they leave. Alternatively, you can simply wedge a stone under one corner of the pen and wait until some birds have left, or you can do as I do and just open the door, let some birds out and then shut it again quickly. There have been occasions when I was not quick enough and the phased release became a general release, but even so the birds have always come back to the pen. One very dry summer the poults actually scratched a hole while dust-bathing, which allowed a dozen or so to squeeze out under the side of the pen. It was as good a way as any of organising a trickle release, except that the hole would also have allowed a stoat, mink or rat to get in to the pen, with potentially disastrous consequences.

If your partridge pens are sited on arable land and you are fortunate enough not to have a fox problem, all you may need is a simple pen to hold the birds until they are all released. If you are turning them out in fields or on a hill where there are sheep and cattle grazing you will be well advised to set up an outer perimeter to prevent the animals from scratching against the sides of the pen and scaring the inhabitants, or worse, collapsing the pen altogether. If you run a short length of stock fence around the pen about 5–10 yards out from it, you will also have a convenient corral in which to locate the outer feeders, drinkers and shelter, out of reach of farm stock. If you supplement the stock fence with an electric fence you should also discourage foxes, sheepdogs and the like and thus provide your poults with a fairly safe area to roost at nights and rest during the day.

Equipment

Whether you are releasing partridges or pheasants you will need feeders and drinkers for them to use while they are in the pen. There are plenty of custom-made units on the market if your budget will run to them, although most shoots tend to save money by making their own, particularly if they have ready access to a supply of metal or plastic drums. It is not difficult to make an effective feeder or drinker, although you can be as elaborate in your design as you wish.

To start with, a word of warning. Most of us can get hold of second-hand 5-, 10- or 40-gallon drums. But you *must* make absolutely sure that they are properly washed out before you fill them with food or water for your poults. A friend lost 300 poults on the first night he put them in the release pen, simply because he had not washed out the drums he was using for drinkers. There was only a trace of chemicals left in them, but it was enough. Clean them thoroughly, and if you are at all doubtful about what was in them before you inherited them, then do not use them at all. Drums are cheap; poults are relatively expensive.

To make a drinker, take a 5- or 10-gallon drum and fill it with water. Then take a 40-

gallon plastic drum and cut the top and bottom off to give you two flat trays about 3 or 4 inches deep and up-end the water-filled drum in one of the trays. The water will flow out until it covers the mouth of the drum, and then it will stop until the birds have drunk enough to let more air in the drum. You can adjust the depth by wedging the drum up on a couple of stones, and all you have to do is top up the drum from time to time. But let me give you a word of warning. If you have several hundred pheasants in a release pen during a hot summer, they will drink an awful lot of water. As a rough guide, 1,000 poults might get through 10 gallons of water a day – possibly even a bit more – and as a gallon of water weighs 10 pounds, that means they will require 100 pounds of water every day. If there is no reliable supply close to the pen you are going to have to transport that water to the pen, and if getting to the pen involves a ½-mile walk across the fields you will find yourself developing very long arms by the time the poults start to leave the pen and make their own drinking arrangements.

Going round the pen topping up a lot of individual drinkers is also quite time-consuming. There is a good case to be made for investing in purpose-built, gravity-fed drinkers and connecting them up to a central reservoir with plastic tubing. A 40-gallon drum mounted on a platform serves well as the reservoir, but make sure you can reach up easily to tip your drums of water in when topping up. Then all you have to do is to keep the reservoir full. If you can get hold of an old bowser, mounted on a trailer, you will make the job of transporting water a lot easier – provided of course, that you can drag the bowser up to the pen. If not, you are back to carrying 5-gallon drums of water across the fields. Incidentally, site the reservoir near the gate to the pen. We built a drinker system in one of our release pens, and for some reason which escapes me, put the reservoir right in the middle of the pen. Now, if the ground is hard enough, I can drive right up to the pen gate, but I then have to carry the drums of water an extra 100 yards or so to reach the reservoir. We will be moving it this summer.

You will not want to have to pour gallons of water every day through a tiny bung-hole in the top of your 40-gallon reservoir drum, so either find a drum with a removable top, or simply cut the top off. You could leave it open, but there is a danger of the poults falling in and drowning, so either make a top from the cut-off end of another drum, or cover the open end with wire netting. This will allow the rain to supplement your own supply of water, which is good, but it will also allow the poults to perch on top of the drum and foul the water, which is not.

To make the simplest kind of feeder you can take a 5- or 10-gallon drum, cut some slots in it with a saw or an angle grinder, fill it with wheat and hang it from a tree about a foot above the ground. You can pour the wheat in through the bung hole, using a funnel – a traffic cone cut down to size works well – to avoid undue spillage, but it is much quicker and easier if you can get hold of drums with removable lids. The slots, cut in the sides or the base, will allow the birds access to the feed, although if you make the slots too wide all the wheat will run out, and if they are too narrow the birds will not be able to feed. Moreover if the slots are in the side the rain will get in and soak the wheat unless you have the feeder under some sort of shelter. There are various ways of letting wire mesh of some kind into the base of the drum for the pheasants to peck the wheat through, although we find that the local badgers quickly become adept at ripping out the mesh to get at the wheat.

The Game Conservancy will sell you 'letter-box' feeders which can be let into the sides

A partridge release pen. It is quite small with feeders inside and out and top netting to keep the birds in until they are ready for release.

of a drum. These allow the birds to peck out the wheat through a slit which is protected from the rain by an angled flap above the slit. These are excellent, but a little expensive. You can make something similar by cutting a hole in either side of a plastic drum to accommodate a length of plastic guttering, fitted upside down. If you extend the guttering 3 or 4 inches beyond the edge of the drum it will keep the rain out of the feed, while the length inside the drum will prevent the wheat or pellets from simply pouring out through the hole.

As I have said, you can simply hang the feeders from a tree or from a couple of posts. The ground immediately underneath will become very wet and muddy during the winter, although a regular scattering of straw will help, as well as giving the birds somewhere to scratch. But if you can find the time to fit legs to your feeders you will be much more flexible in siting them, and will also be able to move them around regularly to prevent the ground getting too bare and muddy. If deer or badgers are a problem you may be able to discourage them by running a short length of fence round your feeding stations, although it is very difficult to stop a determined badger or roe buck, particularly when there is a free meal in the offing.

Hand-feeding daily on straw rides would be the first choice of many shoots if they had time to do it, and indeed, many full-time keepers do just that. You can approximate this system by putting in straw rides with four or five feeders spread along them. When you fill the feeders you can also scatter some wheat on the ride, the idea being that the birds will scratch about in the straw, but will still have food available when the wheat you scattered has been used up. It is a little more wasteful than straight hopper feeding because a lot of wild birds will also take advantage of the free meal, but you may well not mind helping to keep chaffinches, yellowhammers, robins, blue tits and the like alive through the cold weather. You will also find crows and pigeons at the food, which may be a less welcome sight!

For those who like gadgets, there are various feeders on the market which operate electrically with a timer and a device for scattering a measured amount of food at pre-set intervals. These can be excellent for simulating hand-feeding, with the added advantage that the birds do not become too tame through seeing a human with a feed bag every day. On the other hand, they are also quite expensive, especially if you have twenty or thirty feeding stations, and are obviously liable to mechanical and electrical breakdowns, and prone to vandalism. That said, the odd one in more remote corners of the shoot may be an ideal solution to feeding coverts where access is difficult, and they can be especially useful at keeping a flight pond topped up with a little barley each evening.

You can try various other ways of keeping your birds fed and amused. If you can arrange to grow some cereal and have it cut and baled complete – i.e. with the ears still on the straw – you could create straw rides with the food already in place. Bales like these placed in the coverts with the strings cut, but without the straw being scattered, would keep pheasants amused for some time, scratching and pecking and slowly spreading the straw about. Several companies make feed blocks for pheasants, which are basically oversized versions of those sold to feed garden birds. Made from seeds and grain bound together with fat, and possibly containing some kind of spice to attract the pheasants, they will last for several days, or even weeks, depending on the number of birds using them. Some keepers swear by them, others find them of little use. It is worth experimenting with a limited number to see how well they work on your shoot, although I would be reluctant to build my whole feeding strategy around them until I was sure that they would work properly on my ground.

The most important thing about feeding your birds, whether they are pheasants, partridges or ducks, is that there must be a constant supply of food. If you allow the feeders to become empty you can hardly expect your birds to hang about waiting until you get round to refilling them. There may be other feeders, but game birds can be quite territorial, and it may not be a simple matter of the birds from the empty feeding site wandering along to join their friends at the next one. They will almost certainly wander, but it may be in the wrong direction, and they could end up right off the shoot.

6 Rearing for Release

So far we have looked at restocking the shoot with the assumption that the stocking process will begin with poults at the release pen stage, i.e. seven- or eight-week-old pheasants, or eight- to ten-week-old partridges. You can, of course, begin your restocking programme earlier in the production cycle, buying in day-old chicks, setting eggs in an incubator or under a broody hen, or even further back by catching up parent stock and organising a laying pen. You do not have to take on this work – there are plenty of game farms ready and willing to supply you with poults – but you may prefer to produce your own, provided that you have the time and the space to do so.

In many cases, particularly if you have an employer to satisfy or a business to run in addition to your shoot duties, getting everything prepared to receive your poults and then looking after them on a daily basis will be more than enough extra work to keep you busy through the spring and summer. You can order your birds through a game farm and take delivery around the date of your choice, no matter whether you are starting off with 100 birds or with 10,000. You will be entitled to expect them to arrive in good condition and free of disease, and if for some reason they do not, then you will have grounds to seek some form of compensation from your supplier. If you are using a reliable game farm there should be no problems, and if the worst did happen through no fault of yours, your supplier would undoubtedly put things right by refunding your money or providing replacement poults.

But for this reassurance, you will be required to reach into your pockets and dispense a good proportion of your shoot budget. The cost of poults varies, but as we have seen, at the time of writing a pheasant poult ready for the release pen costs anything from £2.50 to £3, with partridge poults being a little more expensive at £3–£4 each. You may be able to find poults for less, or indeed you may be paying more, but the range is close enough for our purposes. Generally, the more birds you are buying the cheaper you should be able to get them. Thus, if you are releasing 100 pheasants you will probably pay about £300 for your poults: if you are releasing 10,000 you might be looking at an outlay of £25,000-plus. In either case, those birds are likely to represent a major portion of your variable costs for the season.

A game farmer, like any other supplier, is in business to make a profit. You can therefore assume that whatever you pay for your poults will be a little more than they cost the game farm. Why, then, should you not produce your own poults, and reduce your shoot costs accordingly?

This is a simple enough question, but not surprisingly, there is no simple answer. The first thing to understand is that you will not necessarily be able to produce poults at a lower cost than the price you pay a game farm. You *may* be able to do so, but there is no guarantee.

You could find that your home-grown poults prove considerably more expensive than those bought ready for release. This might not be a problem if, for example, you reared 100 poults in the back yard and found, when you added things up at the end of the season, that they had actually cost you £350 instead of the £300 you could have paid the game farm. If, however, you hatched and reared 10,000 poults only to find that you could have saved 50p per head by buying them in from the game farm at seven weeks, you will be looking at an extra outlay of £5,000 for the season.

It gets worse. If you had invested several thousand pounds in incubators, rearing units, laying pens, brooders, drinkers, feeders, a generator and a hatchery building in order to rear those 10,000 poults, you may be effectively 'locked in' to continuing to hatch and rear your own, expensive birds, or standing a considerable loss when you dispose of the equipment on the second-hand market. You may be able to operate more efficiently as you gain experience, or to increase the scale of your operation and offset some of the cost by supplying other shoots, although this will not be likely if your costs remain higher than those of the other suppliers.

You should also consider the question of risk. If you buy poults from a game farm you only assume responsibility for these birds when you take delivery of them in a healthy condition. If you are rearing your own you will be liable for the losses if disease wipes out all your chicks, if a fox breaks into your rearing pen and slaughters them, or scatters them to die in the rain, or if the power fails and they all die of cold. You will be responsible if the incubator breaks down and all your eggs fail to hatch, if you set the temperatures wrongly and only get half the chicks you had anticipated, or if you lose all your parent stock from the laying pen and have no eggs to set. Of course, none of these things may happen and you may produce a fine crop of healthy poults with little or no trouble, but it is important to appreciate the extra risks that you take when you decide to produce your own poults instead of buying them in from the game farm. If any of the above disasters strikes the game farm the loss will be theirs, not yours.

Game farms have certain other advantages over the do-it-yourself game rearer. An established business will have learned by its mistakes in previous years. There is a good deal of skill in getting the best performance out of an incubator and in running a brooder house to minimise losses and produce the maximum percentage of strong, healthy poults from a batch of day-old chicks. There are also economies of scale to consider, and the reduction in unit costs achieved by running equipment at its optimum capacity. A brooder will burn very little more gas in keeping 200 poults warm than it will if there are just 50, given the same size of brooder house.

I am not trying to dissuade you from rearing your own poults. There are a number of good reasons why it might be in your best interests to do so. But it is important though that you should appreciate the possible disadvantages in organising your own rearing set-up. Now let us look at the likely advantages.

An overall reduction in shoot costs – or an increase in the numbers you can stock for the same cost – is the most obvious reason for rearing your own poults. As we have seen, the game farm makes a profit; instead of adding to it you could keep it yourself. And if you organise things properly and manage to avoid all the potential disasters, then you may well make a considerable saving. As for the risks involved, your overall risk will certainly be increased, but then the whole business of running a shoot involves risk. If you rely on wild birds you are at enormous risk from the weather and from predators. Even if you buy in

Broody hens can be used to rear pheasants, partridges or, as in this case, ducks.

poults your risks are only decreased, not eliminated. The healthy poults you receive from the game farm could be decimated in one night of driving rain, or in one nocturnal visit from fox, mink, cat, dog or poacher.

Your potential saving can be considerably higher than the margin of profit made by the game farm. Let us consider an example of relatively low-scale production. On the one hand you could order 200 pheasant poults from the game farm and pay £500 for them when they arrive. Now suppose that you catch up ten hen pheasants and a couple of cock birds at the end of the season, clip their wings and house them in an old hen run, where they obligingly produce an average of twenty-five eggs per hen. You can take those 250 eggs and distribute them under a dozen broody hens or bantams which you have begged or borrowed for a couple of months. Given a reasonable hatching rate and a successful rearing period you could produce 200 poults for the cost of half a dozen bags of feed at £10 a bag, plus perhaps a couple of bottles of whisky in return for the loan of the broodies. Let us call it £100 in total. So you will have made an overall saving of £400. I would call that well worth the effort.

It gets better. If you had left those ten hen pheasants out in the wild they might have produced 50–100 chicks for you for nothing, although they might equally well have lost the lot to foxes or crows. When you release them again after you have collected your eggs there is still a chance that they might build a nest and produce a few extra free chicks for the shoot – and even if they do not, you will still have saved £400.

I have not made any allowances for your labour in these calculations. There will be the time you spend in catching up the parent stock, looking after them in the laying pen and collecting the eggs, tending the 'broodies' and in feeding the chicks. You will probably have done all that in a few spare minutes each day, or perhaps delegated the job to your wife or children. Strictly speaking we should cost out those few minutes when counting the cost of the poults, but in practice we can ignore them. So you will have stocked the shoot for one fifth of the cost of buying in poults, and probably got a little quiet satisfaction out of the deal along the way, when you found the first egg, heard the first chick tapping at the shell or watched the 'broodies' mothering their fostered offspring. There are more rewards than monetary ones in producing your own poults.

In the old days broody hens were used extensively by keepers for producing pheasant poults. Looking after ten 'broodies' can be an interesting diversion, but looking after 200–300 – always supposing that you could lay your hands on them in the first place – is more like very hard work. When you consider that the old keepers had to make their own feed for the chicks by boiling up various mixtures of eggs, rabbits and meal, not to mention trapping the rabbits to begin with, you will appreciate that running a rearing field at the turn of the century was not a job for the idle, nor for those who believed in working office hours and a five-day week.

You might not be able to find broody hens. Indeed, even if you can, the modern, hybrid hen is a far less reliable mother than the older breeds, and is quite liable to give up sitting halfway through the incubation period. The alternative is an incubator, and you can buy these in any size you like, from tiny models that will stand in the corner of a garage and hatch out twenty or thirty eggs at a time to large room-sized machines that will churn out chicks by the thousand. If you do not have hens to keep the chicks warm and dry you will have to provide heat with a gas, oil or electric brooding lamp, and shelter in the form of a brooding shed. Again, for twenty or thirty chicks this could be a tiny enclosure in one corner of a shed or garage, but if you are thinking in terms of hundreds or thousands of birds then you will need a proper brooding unit, and probably several of them.

If you only want to produce a few – or a few hundred – poults then you may well be able to do it for a fraction of the cost of bought-in birds, largely because the operation is small enough to ignore labour costs, and not to require any real investment in equipment. An incubator in the corner of a garage, an old hut pressed into service as a brooder shed and a pen on the back lawn may be more than adequate for a small number of chicks, but you will quickly reach a point where proper equipment is essential. Once this happens the potential savings will fall. If you go further, and start to spend so much time running the rearing operation that you need to cost that time at a realistic rate, then the unit savings will be greatly diminished.

Even if you are only going to put down 100 birds in the first place, the total amount that you will save is likely to be no more than £100–£150. Does that size of a saving justify the amount of work that you will have to put into the rearing project? Even if you do not cost the time, you must also consider what other work around the shoot you might have done instead of dealing with incubators and brooders, or with broody hens. Only you can decide whether rearing a few birds is a good option or not.

At the opposite end of the scale, with everything from labour to fuel and depreciation of equipment costed in, you might find that your potential savings were in the order of 30–50p per poult. If you stock your release pens with 10,000 poults then there is a possible saving of anything from £3,000 to £5,000, which might well justify the risk and the initial outlay. Again, you must consider what other work might be neglected in order to run such an extensive rearing programme, although with a turnover of perhaps £20,000 you might well employ temporary labour specifically to run the hatchery and rearing operation. The next logical step from here is to produce a surplus and sell it on to offset some of your own costs – at which point you will be in competition with your local game farm.

While releasing poults is a relatively straightforward matter, the hatching and rearing of chicks requires a lot more thought. There are a whole series of options open to you if you decide to start a rearing programme. You can begin your involvement at any stage – with laying stock, with eggs or with day-old chicks – and you can even skip one or two stages along the way.

You can buy in day-old chicks from a game farm and restrict yourself to rearing them, or you can purchase eggs rather than chicks and start at the incubation stage. The next step backwards in the production chain is the laying pen, but there are still several alternative routes between catching up the adults and releasing the chicks into the brooder units.

You may be able to take the hens you catch up and pass them along to the game farm in return for an agreed number of eggs or chicks per hen. Obviously, the quid pro quo for the game farm is that the hen will produce more eggs than they will return to you. Alternatively, you can put the adult pheasants into your own laying pen and supply the game farm with eggs. The pay-off might be agreed as a certain number of chicks per hundred eggs supplied, or you might employ the hatchery to custom hatch your eggs in return for a fee, or for a percentage of the chicks. What is feasible will depend on the way in which the game farm runs its business: whether they require any hens or eggs from outside sources, whether they operate a custom-hatching service or not, and whether they will provide chicks in return for eggs.

Catching Up

If you are starting out with a new shoot and very little wild game then this is not going to be an option for you. If you want to establish a laying pen but do not have the wild stock to fill it you should contact a local keeper who may have birds to spare and see if you can work out some sort of deal involving laying stock in return for a share of the eggs. Of course, you may already have contacts from beating, picking up or shooting on local shoots in which case you may be able to scrounge a few birds against favours done in the past or promised for the future.

Let us assume, however, that you have a stock of birds on the ground and want to catch up enough to fill your laying pen. The sooner you start catching up the better, if only because a catcher set in early January will be collecting its birds from a much bigger population. If you wait until the end of the season you will have shot over the ground another three or four times, if not more, and there will be fewer birds to catch from, with a correspondingly higher chance that those birds which have survived may have been pricked by a pellet during one of the shoots.

The catcher is simply a cage of some sort with a funnel-type entrance which will allow the birds to get in but not out. You entice them to enter by scattering food in and around the cage. If you set the cage out on a feed ride for a week or so before you want to start collecting your layers, and open one end or prop up a corner to allow the birds free access, you should find it easier to get your numbers when you begin to trap in earnest. Obviously, once the trap is in catching mode you must visit it regularly – at least once a day and preferably more often – so that the birds are not unduly stressed, nor exposed to danger from vermin or poachers. Partridges can be caught in much the same way as pheasants.

Pheasants can be caught up in the spring to stock the laying pens.

Sport in the Highlands. The scenery is superb, but most Highland estates will run at a loss.

Pheasants on a feed ride. Many other wild birds will benefit from the food provided for the pheasants.

A peregrine falcon is just one of the predators which will compete for your shootable surplus of game.

Grouse over pointers. As much of the pleasure of a shoot comes from the surroundings as from the actual shooting.

Strip-burning heather to improve the moorland for grouse and other birds of the open hill.

Red-legged or French partridge.

Releasing just a few pheasants can provide good sport for a very modest cost.

Snipe and partridge in the bag show a modest return from a day's shooting over bird dogs.

The red grouse is found only in Britain and Ireland and is arguably the best of all sporting birds.

The goshawk is making a comeback from the depredations of DDT and Dieldrin poisoning.

A cock pheasant – a prime target for many predators both furred and feathered.

A rearing set-up: a brooding shed with gas heater and a covered run leading to an open area for the poults to harden off.

Some guns will appreciate the chance to rest and recuperate during the lunch break.

Good dogs, like this cocker spaniel, are vital to find and flush game ahead of the beating line.

Guns moving into a forestry belt. Grants for softwoods are lower than those for broadleaved woodlands.

Old-fashioned farming methods may have been slow and inefficient but they were far more sympathetic to the needs of wildlife.

Heading for home, tired but happy at the end of a long day on the hill

Grouse shooting over an Irish setter on a hot day in August. Once the trees develop, this ground will no longer hold grouse.

Driven pheasant shooting in the Scottish Borders on a crisp winter morning.

Indeed, once one partridge has found its way into a pen the family instinct of the rest of the covey may well lead to them all incarcerating themselves along with it.

The Laying Pen

Pheasants and partridges require different management once they have been caught. Where the pheasant is polygamous and can be penned with one cock to six or eight hens the partridge prefers to pair off and set up home as it were in a family unit. One problem which is fundamental to pairing partridges is ensuring that your 'pair', if you are placing a single pair in each pen rather than using a large pen with a number of birds penned together, actually consists of one male and one female. No other combination will do. Two cocks will fight, and two hens may lay plenty of eggs but not produce any chicks. Sexing partridges is easy in theory, although not necessarily so in practice. The grey partridge cock has more orange on his head than the female and the horseshoe on his chest is usually more strongly marked. Redlegs are harder to tell apart, although the cock is generally heavier than the hen, and may also have signs of a spur on the back of his legs. Even if you cannot tell them apart the partridges themselves will make no mistakes, so watch their behaviour closely once you put them in the pens.

If you are hoping to produce a large number of partridges you might consider copying the commercial producers and using raised pens with wire mesh floors. However, if you are just aiming to produce a hundred or two you can build your laying pens out of the same sections that you will use for the release pens, not forgetting a top net of course. A shelter which will double up as a dusting area, a feeder and a drinker, and a box full of sand for the birds to lay in, will pretty much complete the requirements.

A laying pen for pheasants can be of any size. If you use a small pen, made up from four 8–12-foot sections, you can house one cock and eight or ten hens per pen, and move the pen onto clean ground every few days. It will have a top net to keep the birds in and the predators out. At the opposite end of the scale you can pen a lot of birds in a big open-topped pen – one of your release pens perhaps – provided that you brail their wings so that they cannot fly out. House them in the same ratio of one cock to eight to ten hens, and provide them with plenty of cover to lay their eggs under. All you have to do then is to ensure that you can find the eggs.

In between these two options, you could have a pen perhaps 10–12 yards square, covered with a top net, and with perhaps three or four cocks and twenty to twenty-five hens. If you can make it bigger and still cover it with a top net then so much the better. The top net is not just to keep the pheasants in but also to keep crows, magpies and the like out, which will save both your eggs and your pheasants' pellets. Worm the birds in plenty of time before they start laying and do not try to skimp on their diet. Use a proper layers' pellet designed for game birds which will give them the best possible chance of producing a good number of fertile eggs while maintaining their condition for when you release them back into the wild.

Collect the eggs regularly – at least once a day and preferably more often – clean them as soon as you have collected them, and store them in a cool, dark place. The sooner they are transferred to the incubator the better, as the longer they are stored the lower the hatchability is likely to be.

Incubation

If you are planning to use broody hens or bantams to incubate your eggs you can safely leave all the technical aspects of incubation, such as temperature and humidity control and frequency of turning the eggs, to them. You will have to provide them with some sort of secure nesting accommodation – secure from foxes, cats and the like – and ensure that they are fed and watered; the 'broodies' should do the rest. If your 'broodies' are housed in traditional coops you will have to make time to see that they come out at least once a day to eat, evacuate their bowels and stretch their legs. You might like to do the same if your birds are sitting in a shed or barn, but the chances are that they will see to all these things quite adequately without you. Bantams in particular are experts at slipping off into the countryside somewhere, disappearing for three weeks or so, and then turning up again with a straggle of tiny chicks behind them. They seem to manage quite well on their own in these circumstances, so it is debatable how much human interference is really required. However, it may keep you happy to become more directly involved, particularly if you are one of those people who feels the need to be doing something rather than letting nature take its course.

Mechanical incubation is a rather different proposition. What a broody hen can do simply by sitting still for three weeks or so requires considerable skill and no small amount of machinery if man is to achieve comparable results. If you are planning to hatch out the eggs yourself rather than entrusting the job to a 'broody' or to a commercial hatchery, then you must be sure to follow the instructions which come with your incubator, and follow them *precisely*. A tiny variation in temperature can have a disastrous effect on the percentage of eggs which hatch.

Unless you already have some experience with incubators, or perhaps have access to one and are only planning to produce a few chicks, it might be best to leave the incubation process to the professionals. Taking a series of hatches from a small incubator will mean that you will be producing your chicks in a wide mixture of ages and sizes, while investing in a large enough machine to produce all your requirements in one hatch will mean that it will stand idle for forty-eight weeks each year. You could of course start hatching eggs for other shoots, but this is leading us into the realms of game farming rather than shoot management, and you will probably be more than busy enough running your own shoot to have time to be thinking about providing chicks and poults for the neighbours.

Rearing

The rearing phase involves taking day-old chicks from the incubator and raising them to seven or eight weeks old in the case of pheasants, and a week or two older for partridges, before moving them to the release pens. If you buy poults from the game farm this stage will have been done for you, and obviously you will have to pay for the work involved. Typically, a seven-week-old pheasant poult might cost around £3, as we have seen, whereas a day-old chick could be bought for about £1. The rearing of chicks in quantity is quite labour-intensive, so there is a considerable saving to be made by doing it yourself if you have the time and the necessary facilities.

We will look at the equipment you need in a moment, but first a word of warning. Rearing your birds from day old should enable you to save a proportion of your costs, but

A rearing set-up: a brooding shed with gas heater and a covered run leading to an open area for the poults to harden off.

it will also mean that you expose your operation to a greater proportion of the risks. Chicks can die from cold and wet, from overheating, from attacks by vermin and from any one of a number of diseases. When you buy poults, the game farm will have assumed, and presumably overcome, these risks. Once you have taken delivery of your day-old chicks, however, they are your problem, and if the brooder fails on a cold night, the roof blows off the shed and the rain gets in, a passing cat slaughters all your chicks or a dose of fowl pest wipes them out, then you have to stand the loss. None of these might happen – indeed they probably will not happen if you are clean and conscientious in your chick husbandry – but they might, and for a certain number of rearers every year something does go wrong.

If you used a broody hen to hatch out your eggs you will presumably use her to rear the chicks as well. This can be an excellent option if you are dealing with small numbers as the hen, while acting as a surrogate mother, will impart a certain amount of what social workers call 'life skills' to the chicks. You can simply surround the coop with a few pen sections to give the chicks a limited amount of freedom, then move them on to clean ground as they need it. This is arguably a far better way to rear chicks than using heated brooding sheds, covered runs and the like, but it is not an option available to everyone, particularly if you are thinking of rearing several hundred – or several thousand – chicks rather than just a few dozen.

The basic rearing process is simple enough in theory. The day-old chicks need to be kept warm and dry with easy access to food and water. As they grow older they will gradually need less heat and more space, with increasing access to the open air. The chicks are progressively 'hardened off' during the seven weeks or so between hatching and releasing, so that by the time they are moved out to the release pen they should be able to survive life in the open. You would not release them in the teeth of a summer gale or a downpour of monsoon proportions of course – if you do, you can expect to lose a good many of them – but given well-hardened poults and a decent few days' weather you should not have too many problems – in theory.

The standard layout for a rearing unit for pheasants consists of three parts. The chicks start off in a brooder unit. This is an enclosed hut heated by a gas or electric brooder lamp. In the first few days it is usual to confine the chicks to the area under the brooder by using a roll of cardboard or something similar and then increasing their space as they settle into their new home. The temperature is controlled by raising or lowering the lamp which is hung directly over the chicks. If you find the chicks huddled under the lamp it means they are too cold and it should be lowered; if they are spread all round the walls it means they are too hot. It is essential that in the first few days the lamp does not go out for any length of time, so ensure that you have plenty of gas, and beware of electricity cuts.

Adjoining the brooder house should be a small, covered run where the chicks can gain their first experience of the outside world without actually being exposed to the driving rain and gale-force winds that so often pass for summer in Britain. The third stage is a large, open pen where they can run about on the grass. This pen should be netted over, and the grass should be kept short so that the poults do not get wet and chilled if they are out in the run after rain.

The size of the set-up will depend on the number of birds you are planning to rear, and to some extent on the space and materials you have available. The Game Conservancy recommend the following dimensions for a unit to rear 100 pheasant chicks: a brooder section 5 feet square for starting the chicks off, a covered run about twice this size – say 10 feet by 5 – and an outer, open pen a minimum of 20 feet square. Note that for the open run the dimension is the *minimum* space needed, and the larger this can be made the better

The covered run with drinker, gas brooder and free access to the open pen.

so that the ground is less prone to fouling and puddling.

If you are rearing a lot of chicks it is better to have several small units rather than one giant one. The danger of disease spreading through the birds is slightly reduced if they are not all housed together, and smaller units are easier to move on to fresh ground if they are used for more than one crop. If you have ten units with 100 birds in each and one brooder lamp fails then only one tenth of your stock will be at risk. If the whole 1,000 are in one hut when the bulb fuses or the gas runs out there is a danger that you will lose the whole lot.

There is a great deal of common sense involved in rearing chicks to the release stage. The chicks themselves will provide plenty of hints, particularly if they are too hot, too cold or too cramped in their quarters. They should not be introduced to the covered run when there is a gale blowing draughts through every chink in the fencing nor, should you pick a cold, rainy afternoon to open the door to the outer run. Your problems may not concern cold and wet, however; it is quite possible that the biggest danger to your chicks will come from dehydration and heat exhaustion. If your rearing programme does coincide with drought and heatwave conditions your growing chicks might benefit from a gentle – and I do mean gentle – spray from a hose while they are out in the run. This will both cool them and help with the hardening-off process.

It hardly needs to be said that feeders and drinkers should start off scrupulously clean, and be kept clean throughout the rearing programme. Remove any dead chicks as soon as you see them and dispose of them properly: do not just toss them over the hedge to encourage rats and other vermin to take an interest in your pens.

You may have to set up anti-vermin measures around the pens to kill or discourage a variety of predators. Foxes, dogs, cats, stoats, weasels, rats, mink and badgers can all create havoc if they once gain entry to the rearing complex. An electric fence around the perimeter is probably the best way to start discouraging the larger predators. A good, sharp sting on the nose can have a salutary effect on foxes and their ilk and, if properly charged and maintained, may well keep them from ever taking a close interest in your birds. Nearer the pens a few tunnel traps can account for the smaller killers such as stoats and rats, although if you have a major problem with rats it should be dealt with by the proper distribution of poisoned bait, preferably some time before your chicks begin to hatch. Rats will not only kill the chicks and take eggs from the laying pens and from wild birds; they will also steal and foul the food, carry disease to the chicks (and possibly to you and your dogs), and generally create mess and destruction in their wake. The rat is most certainly a visitor to the shoot that you should not tolerate.

Instead of building rearing units specifically to house your chicks you may prefer to make use of such existing buildings as are available to you. Old stables or byres, loose boxes, pig sties, chicken huts and the like can all be adapted to rear chicks and, although generally less satisfactory than a purpose-built rearing unit, they can be perfectly adequate to bring your birds from day old through to the release stage. Any building you decide to use should be well ventilated but free from draughts, at least in the area where the day-old chicks will be started off. You may be able to improve the microclimate considerably with temporary surrounds made from cardboard or plywood to keep the chicks close under the brooder lamp.

It is absolutely vital that whatever building you are planning to use is thoroughly cleaned before the chicks are introduced. This is particularly important if the building has

previously housed other poultry, which may have left some form of disease lurking in it. You will probably have to adapt your rearing plan to suit the building, unless you are lucky enough to have something available that can easily provide a brooding area, a covered pen and an outside run. If you have, then you can raise your chicks along the lines of those in a purpose-built rearing unit. If not, then you must adapt.

You may decide to rear the chicks indoors for the first three weeks or so, until they no longer need the warmth of the brooder lamp, and then transfer them to an outside run with a shelter for cover from rain and wind, and for the birds to roost in at night. This can work well provided you are careful with the timing of the move from brooder shed to outside run and do not suddenly expose the young birds to a summer hailstorm. It helps if you can begin getting them accustomed to rain before you move them by gently spraying them with a fine mist of water on hot days, just as you might for birds in the run during a heatwave.

If it is not feasible to put a shelter in the outside run, you can even rear the chicks right through to the release stage inside a covered shed. Good ventilation and plenty of space are even more important where the chicks are to be kept inside for the full rearing period, as is the artificial hardening-off provided by misting them with a hose each day. It is not the ideal way to rear chicks but it can work given proper care and attention to detail. A custom-built rearing unit is the ideal, but the cost savings achieved by using an existing structure may – and I emphasise *may* – make it worth while following some alternative route.

Partridges present slightly different problems to pheasants when it comes to rearing.

Poults spreading out and hardening off in the open part of their run.

Grey partridges are not easy to manage, and can be extremely lively. One keeper swore that the only way to deal with a shed full of grey partridge chicks was to keep them in semi-darkness for much of the time and harden them off with a regular spray from a hose prior to release. Greys need a very high-protein diet and you should ensure that the food you are supplied with is properly formulated with them in mind and is not ordinary pheasant or poultry chick crumb.

Redlegs are considerably easier than greys, being less prone to hysteria and generally more tractable. Both types will normally be kept in the rearing unit for a few weeks longer than pheasant chicks and, with their faster rate of maturing, will be close to young adults when they are released at about ten weeks. They can fly like adults at this stage too, and will quickly grow to their full size and speed of flight once released. This faster rate of maturing is the reason why partridge shooting begins on 1 September whereas most pheasant shoots do not start in earnest until late October or early November.

Feather-pecking

Feather-pecking is the problem you are most likely to experience with your pheasant chicks. It may be caused by boredom, by a lack of something in the birds' diet, or indeed by a lack of something in their brains, but whatever the cause, an outbreak of feather-pecking can have very serious consequences. There are two ways to stop it: by cutting off the end of the upper beak or by fitting a plastic or metal bit into the birds' nostrils. If you clip the beak it will grow back naturally; if you use bits you will have to remove them all when you put the birds out to the release pen or use biodegradable bits that will weaken and fall out naturally after a few weeks.

Beak-clipping or bitting will both inflict a certain amount of stress on the birds, although not nearly as much as a severe outbreak of feather-pecking. Ideally you should manage to get your birds through to the release point without feather-pecking and without having to clip or bit them, and many rearers do so. If you decide not to clip or bit as a precautionary measure, then you should keep a very close watch for the first signs of feather-pecking and be ready to act immediately if it does occur.

Feather-pecking can also start after the poults have been released, and thus when you cannot do anything about it. If you do spot signs in the release pen – drops of blood on the ground or birds with bleeding feather follicles – you may be able to minimise the damage by devising ways to keep the poults occupied until they spread out away from the pen. Boredom may well be a factor, particularly if they are fed from hoppers which allow them to fill their crops quickly and easily. Straw rides for them to scratch about on, bunches of greenery for them to peck and a feeding system that makes them work for their food can all help, although if your poults are absolutely determined to feather-peck it will be very difficult to stop it altogether.

Diseases

Where the same release pen is used for several seasons there is a danger that disease or parasites can become established, ready to infect the next crop of birds. Perhaps the most common problem in the release pen is an outbreak of gapes, which is caused by a parasite, the gapeworm. This infests the windpipe of the poults and causes them to make a characteristic wet, snicking noise, with the head held up and the beak open. If left

unchecked it can quickly run through the whole pen, killing some birds and leaving others badly weakened.

    The worm is passed to the birds via snails, slugs, earthworms and the like and can lie dormant in the ground from one season to the next. In theory you can sterilise the soil with some form of disinfectant. In practice this is likely to prove impossible when dealing with a release pen, but obviously you should ensure that brooder huts and the like are thoroughly clean at the start of each season. You can treat gapes and other parasitic worms by using a remedy provided by your vet which is added to the poults' food or water. This is most easily done while the chicks are still in the rearing unit, where you have complete control over their food and drink, and may be worth considering as a preventative measure just prior to release. If you have an outbreak once the birds have begun to leave the release pen it is far more difficult to ensure that every bird is treated.

    There is a whole range of diseases that can affect your chicks and poults, and in many cases it requires an expert to identify them correctly and prescribe the proper treatment. If you start finding dead birds with no obvious explanation for their deaths, or if your birds look listless and generally down, it is well worthwhile consulting your local vet or a keeper with more experience. In many cases a disease may be easily treatable if it is caught early but almost impossible to eradicate once it has taken a firm hold. A visit to the vet and a post-mortem examination is not cheap, but it will certainly be cheaper than replacing several hundred dead poults if there really is a serious problem in the offing.

Mallard can be easy to rear but it may be difficult to show them to their best advantage if they become too tame.

In Conclusion

Hatching and rearing your own chicks is not something you can tackle in a half-hearted manner. You can produce a few extra birds for your shoot very easily if you have access to a broody hen or two and a few settings of eggs, but producing poults by the hundreds or thousands will take a considerable amount of work. It can be a very satisfying experience seeing the eggs hatch and the chicks quickly turning from tiny balls of fluff into well-feathered poults, and it may save you a proportion of your shoot costs. With the rewards go risks, however, and you should consider the extra work involved, the danger of losing eggs and chicks to predators, disease or power failures, and the loss of time which might have been spent on vermin control or other work around the shoot before deciding to go ahead.

7 Vermin Control

Vermin control, or predator control if you prefer the term, can be one of the more contentious aspects of running a shoot. It is difficult, if not actually impossible, to run a shoot without paying some attention to controlling those predators which will compete with you for the game. Irrationally, the general public may not object to us shooting pheasants, pigeons, grouse, rabbits and the like – although an increasing number seem to object to just about any countryside activity apart from hiking and picnicking – but they may well object to the measures we take to protect our game from predation.

This response is rarely logical and often inconsistent. How many of those who condemn us for killing their 'feathered friends' will keep a cat as a pet? How many of those who consider it reprehensible to kill a stoat or a weasel will have no objection to the killing of a rat? Would those who see the fox as a friendly, furry and altogether delightful animal feel the same way if one came into their garden and ate the children's pet rabbit? Why is it all right for me to kill a crow but somehow wrong for me to shoot a magpie? Presumably it is because the magpie is a far prettier sight with its piebald feathering, long tail and jaunty demeanour, despite the fact that a song-bird chick eaten by the magpie is just as dead as one eaten by the crow.

Few keepers would want to kill the last fox, the last stoat or even the last crow, although they might have less sympathy with the last mink or the last rat. What we should aim to do with our vermin control is to strike a balance – or more correctly, to maintain an imbalance – between our wish to shoot game and the quite natural desire of any predator to live, breed and raise its young. It is that word 'balance' that contains the crux of predator control.

All wild creatures undergo population swings, which can be extremely rapid and short-lived in the case of small creatures like aphids or ladybirds or happen almost imperceptibly over a period of years, even centuries, for the largest animals such as elephants, whales, dinosaurs and of course man. The factors behind these swings in population are often extremely complex, but they will almost certainly involve the availability of food along with other things such as changes in climate or habitat, increasing pollution, natural evolution and so on. There is no enduring balance in nature, our environment is a dynamic system and changes constantly, whether those changes are influenced by man or by other agencies outside our control.

In the short term, when we introduce hundreds or thousands of game birds onto a shoot, we are artificially boosting the food supply for all those creatures which eat partridge or pheasant, and a sudden increase in food availability is likely to be followed by an increase in those creatures which eat that food – unless we do something to limit the increase. And clearly, since it is our intention to crop and eat those game birds ourselves, we cannot allow the local predator population to grow to such an extent that there is eventually no surplus for us to shoot. The only reasonable answer to this is to practise some form of predator control.

It is important to look at predator control in a wider context than the old-fashioned view of simply killing everything which might conceivably have eaten an egg, chick, poult or adult game bird. The methods of the Victorian keepers are roundly condemned by many people today, but it is only fair to view them in the context of the times in which they occurred. Attitudes have changed enormously since the nineteenth century – indeed, they have changed considerably in the latter half of the twentieth century – and an act which was seen as quite normal and even praiseworthy 100 years ago could well see you gracing the cells of one of Her Majesty's prisons today.

The Law

A hundred or more years ago a keeper could do pretty much what he liked as far as predator control was concerned. Shooting, trapping and poisoning were all legal and practically everything that ate – or might be suspected of eating – game was killed out of hand. Indeed, many keepers took matters further, and would also kill birds and animals that they thought might compete for food with their partridges and pheasants. Competition pigeon shooting involved live pigeons, not clay discs, and there are records of men shooting large numbers of sparrows, swallows, larks and even bats for a wager, or just because the poor creatures happened to be there. Public perceptions and attitudes were different then.

Today, a series of parliamentary Acts have severely curtailed what may be done legally in the interests of game preservation. The law now controls what birds and animals may be killed, the times when some of them may be killed, and the methods which may be used to kill them. In many cases it is a criminal offence even to disturb certain creatures, as for example the bats which may be living in your roof space, while you will need a licence to

A ladder-entry crow trap sited in a forestry plantation.

take a photograph of certain birds at their nests. At the same time, while you or I would
be prosecuted for taking a picture of an osprey on its nest because we would be disturbing
it, it is perfectly acceptable for a researcher to climb the tree, remove the chicks so that
they can be weighed and measured, and then replace them in the nest. Presumably being
manhandled by a licensed researcher is less stressful than being photographed from a distance by a common member of the public.

Since so many predators are now protected, keepers have had to find alternatives to
shooting and trapping in order to keep their game safe. Where once the simple answer to
any raptor that showed an interest in the release pen was a pole trap or 1¼ ounces of shot,
any keeper who follows that route today runs a very real risk of prosecution, a fine or a
jail sentence and the loss of his firearms certificate and possibly his job. Instead, we must
seek to deny the predator access to the poults, or perhaps provide it with an alternative
food supply. The RSPB is said to have experimented with scattering dead mice about one
of their reserves in an attempt to prevent hawks killing avocet chicks, although I doubt
whether this approach would work effectively over 10,000 acres of grouse moor. On the
other hand, a buzzard which shows an undue interest in your poults might well respond
to a regular supply of rabbits being placed on a prominent spot near the pen. As yet there
is no law to prevent you killing rabbits.

There is no single Act which codifies the law relating to predator control, nor is the law
static. New legislation, amendments to existing legislation and additions to the list of
those creatures which are afforded legal protection can all mean that something which is
perfectly legal today may be a criminal act tomorrow. It is up to you to make sure that you
keep up to date, since ignorance of the law is not a defence. You are presumed to know

*Detail of the ladder-type
entrance to the crow trap.*

what is and what is not legal. I will refer to some of the main provisions of the various Acts, but remember, what is legal as I write this may not be legal when you read it. If in doubt seek informed advice before you pull a trigger or set a trap: killing a protected bird or animal will see you in court – and possibly in prison – even if you acted in the genuine belief that what you were doing was allowed.

Despite the restrictions placed on keepers by legislation, there are still a number of predators which may be killed, provided that an illegal method is not used. Thus, while there is no law to prevent you killing a mink by shooting it, trapping it in a cage trap or an approved body-grip trap, it would be an offence to catch one in a gin trap or to poison it. At the opposite extreme, it is an offence to kill a protected species by mistake, even if you kill it in an approved trap which was set for a different, and legal, quarry.

The law regarding the protection of birds in particular has changed in recent years. In the past certain birds were protected by Act of Parliament, and anything that was not specifically mentioned was effectively a legal quarry. Now the situation is reversed, and all birds are protected with the exception of those species which an Act of Parliament says may be legally killed – subject, in some cases, to close seasons. The following birds and animals, all of which are to some extent 'enemies' of game may be controlled, although there are often restrictions:

- foxes
- mink
- stoats
- weasels
- grey squirrels
- feral cats
- feral ferrets
- rats
- mice
- crows
- rooks
- magpies
- jays
- jackdaws
- great and lesser black-backed gulls

There are certain other birds such as starlings and sparrows which may be controlled, but which are not likely to pose a threat to your pheasant poults. If you are wondering why I include mice in the list, then I assume you have not yet seen the havoc which they can cause when they get in amongst stocks of wheat or pheasant pellets.

You should note that *all* birds of prey are protected. Hawks, falcons, owls, buzzards, harriers, kites, ospreys and eagles alike enjoy specific and special protection under the Wildlife and Countryside Act, and killing any of them is likely to involve very severe penalties for the guilty party. The fact that they may have been making severe inroads into your chicks, or even your parent stock, is no defence. Equally, badgers, otters, martens and polecats can also wreak havoc around your pens and nesting birds, but you may not take the law into your own hands and trap or shoot them. If a badger starts visiting your release pen your only legal recourse is to find some way to prevent him getting in (which is far from easy), to try to discourage him from visiting in the first place, or, as a last resort, to resite the pen.

Some of the predators can actually be beneficial in the proper context. Stoats and weasels will kill mice and rats as well as game birds and their chicks, while you may even welcome the attentions of the fox around the rabbit warrens if rabbit damage is a significant problem on your shoot. I cannot think of any reason why you might want rats or mink about the place but no doubt some conservationists could come up with a theory to support their presence in the countryside, although it would probably not apply to their own back gardens.

There are a variety of ways in which you can control predators. The direct approach, which we might call the traditional method, is to kill them, by shooting, trapping, snaring, gassing or poisoning. Broadly, if the law permits you to kill a predator you will be within your rights if you shoot it, and you may be permitted to trap it, but you will almost certainly not be allowed to poison it.

Poison may be used to control rats and mice, moles and grey squirrels, but only within strict limits laid down by legislation. The poisoned bait must be laid in such a way that only the intended victims will have access to it. In certain areas where red squirrels still survive as well as greys it is illegal to set poisoned baits for the greys, and even where it is permitted to poison grey squirrels there are strict rules concerning how the poisoned bait must be presented. It is not simply illegal to poison, or attempt to poison, any other species, it is illegal to lay poison where species other than the legal victims might have access to it. You would, for example, be breaking the law if you put out poisoned bait for rats in a place where crows would be likely to find it.

Trapping and snaring are also closely regulated. There are a number of spring trap designs which were approved by the Ministry of Agriculture; all are intended to kill their victims by gripping them across the body or neck. This is the essential difference between the modern, approved trap designs and the old-fashioned, and now strictly illegal, gin trap which was intended to catch the prey by the legs or feet and hold it until the trapper came along to kill it.

Spring traps or body-grip traps are also commonly called tunnel traps, for the obvious reason that they must be set in some form of tunnel which will prevent any animal or bird other than the intended victim from being caught. Some traps are only approved for setting in tunnels, others may be set in rabbit holes, but all must be set underground, or in an artificial tunnel made from wood, stones, bricks, breeze blocks, drain pipes or something similar.

Snares can, in theory, be used to take any of the mammalian predators, although in practice they are employed mainly against foxes and rabbits. It is illegal to use a self-locking snare, and it is incumbent upon the trapper to take every reasonable precaution to ensure that a snare will not trap a protected species instead of the animal it was intended to take. As with other types of trap, you must inspect your snares at least once every day. A fox wire should incorporate a stop on the noose nine inches from the eye so that a fox will be held, but not strangled. This stop will also prevent the snare from tightening fully around the leg of a deer, cow or sheep if one is unfortunate enough to become entangled in the wire. While it is not a specific requirement of the law, it makes sense to put a wire stop on the noose a few inches from the end so that it will not tighten fully around the leg of a deer or sheep if one is unfortunate enough to become entangled in the wire.

Cage traps, which take their prey alive, are particularly useful when there is a danger that a spring trap might end up killing the wrong victim. If you have a problem with grey squirrels in an area which supports reds, with mink on a waterway which also holds an otter population, with feral cats where pet cats might also become victims, or even with foxes in a wood which also has a badger population, then you may be best to consider using a cage trap which will take its victims alive and unharmed, giving you the option of freeing anything which is caught by mistake.

Cage traps are also used against the various members of the crow family. The small, portable types, often referred to as Larsen traps, and the larger, semi-permanent cages are designed to take crows, magpies etc. alive, and generally work best if a live decoy bird is housed in the trap to lure others in. If you do use a live decoy it must have food and fresh water, shelter, and room to spread its wings. As with all cage traps, if you catch a protected bird by mistake you will be able to turn it loose again, unharmed.

Timing of Predator Control

Before we look more closely at *how* to control predators we should spend a few moments considering *when* control is most important.

As far as the wild game on your shoot is concerned, the most vulnerable time of the year is the spring and early summer, when the game birds are nesting, incubating their eggs and rearing their chicks, and the hares and rabbits are raising their young. Eggs, sitting hens and young chicks are especially vulnerable, as are leverets and young rabbits. At the same time, when your stock is most likely to end up being taken, the predators themselves are rearing young and therefore require more food than through the rest of the year.

If you are rearing replacement stock from day old your brooder units and pens are an obvious temptation for all manner of predators. Hundreds or possibly thousands of chicks concentrated into one small area and confined within a pen represent easy hunting and well-fed young for any meat-eating birds or mammals which happen to find them. Properly designed, constructed and maintained pens will deny access to most predators, although it would take a very strong pen to stop a determined badger or even a large dog bent on mischief. At the same time, the fact that the rearing pens will attract the attention of predators can be useful to the keeper, as foxes, rats, stoats, mink and the like which are drawn to the scent and sound of your chicks can be trapped, snared or, in the case of rats, poisoned as they attempt to find a free lunch.

Releasing poults means that the time of greatest danger is put back a couple of months, with the danger zone shifting out to the release pens. The first few days after release are the most dangerous for your poults, when their curiosity has not yet been tempered by a measure of caution and respect for the dangers of the wild after the comparative safety of the rearing units. Again, a well-designed release pen, properly maintained defences, particularly an electric fence, and regular patrols will deter predators or deny them access. As with rearing pens, the release pen will attract vermin and can be used as the giant 'bait' in the centre of a line of snares and traps.

It is not only your game birds which are vulnerable in the spring. Predators are also tied to their nests and dens while incubating eggs or rearing their young. A pair of crows shot or trapped during the nesting season will be as beneficial as half a dozen crows shot later, after they have reared their young. Consequently, although predator control represents a year-round duty for many shoots, it is at its most effective during the early spring and summer months, both in protecting your game and in reducing the overall predator population. A spring blitz on crows and foxes is advisable for all shoots, and absolutely essential for those which rely heavily on wild game to provide their sport.

Corvids

The main enemies of game among the crow family are the carrion crow, its northern cousin the hooded crow and the magpie. Rooks, jackdaws and jays will also rob nests given the chance but they are less dedicated to the task and more content to satisfy their appetites with an alternative food supply. Rooks were once controlled by shooting the young 'branchers' when they first left their nests, and some shoots still do this in the late spring. A whole range of small-calibre, relatively low-powered firearms, known as rook rifles, was made for this specific purpose and for the more general shooting of small game and vermin, although now the ubiquitous .22 rim-fire would be the logical choice of most rook shooters.

The once common method of controlling crows by scattering eggs laced with poison around the shoot is strictly illegal and was in any case extremely dangerous to humans and domestic pets as well as to the intended victims. You may now control your crows only by shooting them or trapping them in some form of cage trap. If you carry a gun with you when you are out and about on the shoot you will almost certainly find some targets, although all the corvids seem to have a remarkable instinct for distinguishing the human who means them harm and keeping well out of shot. If you can find their nests, and if you have the time and the patience, you may be able to shoot the parents as they come in to it.

A typical example of the legal type of spring trap, shown here in the set position . . .

And here sprung. The trap is designed to kill its victims quickly and cleanly.

This is not simply a matter of hiding yourself close to the nest site and waiting, since a crow which has been put off the nest by your approach is unlikely to return until it has seen you leave again. The way to get around this is to have a friend accompany you to the nest and then walk away once you have hidden yourself, the theory being that a crow cannot count and will assume that your companion's departure signals the end of the danger.

Shooting works, provided that you can spare the time to lurk under the nests, but in today's typical forestry plantation it may be impossible to find the nests at all, much less get within gunshot of them. On the other hand, a cage trap, once set up, will be active right through the daylight hours, and will attract even those crows whose nests are totally inaccessible.

There are two versions of the cage trap: a large, fixed trap with a funnel type of entrance which can, if you are lucky, catch a number of crows, rooks etc., in a single day; and the smaller, portable Larsen trap, which has a spring-loaded entrance to its catching compartments, each of which will only catch a single bird since access is denied once the door has been sprung. There are a number of common designs of cage trap, but in essence they all consist of a wire netting cage with either a 'lobster pot' type of funnel entrance, or a ladder type. The object of both is to allow a crow, rook or magpie to drop down into the trap, but to ensure that once inside they will be unable to fly back out.

The Larsen trap is generally divided into two, three or four compartments, one to hold a decoy bird and the others with open doors which will slam shut when a spring is released by the incoming bird's weight acting on some form of trigger. The great advantage of the Larsen trap is that it is easily moved around the shoot. Crows and magpies are extremely cunning. Moving a trap just a few yards may mean the difference between catching crows and not, and it is a lot easier to move a Larsen trap, which can be picked up and carried or put in the back of a pick-up, than it is to disassemble a cage trap, move it section by section to a new location and then assemble it all again.

The best method of attracting crows and magpies to your trap is to use a live decoy. As I have said, a bird used for this purpose must have access to food and water, shelter, and enough room to stretch its wings. Once you have one live crow it should be relatively simple to obtain decoys for your other traps. Getting the first decoy can be a problem, and the best solution is to obtain a live bird from a neighbouring shoot which already has decoys for its traps. Failing that you can bait your traps with eggs, rabbit or lamb carcasses, or even a few slices of white bread, and trust to a mixture of hunger and curiosity to lure your first victim into the trap.

It makes sense to site your traps well away from footpaths and other areas where they might attract the attention of the general public. This is an obvious and sensible precaution with any trap, snare or release pen, but is particularly important with something as large as a cage trap, especially if it contains a decoy bird hopping about and catching the eye of the passer-by. At best you will be accused of cruelty; at worst your traps will be destroyed and your decoy birds liberated.

As with all traps, you should visit your cages at least once per day. If you are unable to do this – perhaps because you can only get to the shoot at weekends – then you can always take your decoy birds home and house them in some sort of pen for the days when you cannot inspect the cages. If your cages attract the wrong sort of predator, be it a buzzard, a sparrow-hawk or a peregrine falcon, then you should turn it loose again, unharmed. It is not unknown for a raptor to be planted in a cage trap with the express intention of catching you in the act of killing a protected species. This may sound like paranoia, but I know of more than one instance when attempts were made to entice keepers into capturing raptors or taking their eggs with the aim of discrediting both the individual keeper and the shooting world as a whole.

Foxes

Apart from the various members of the crow family, the fox is the main predator of game. There may be exceptions; if you own or rent a grouse moor which happens to be blessed with three or four pairs of hen harriers, then they may well be the main enemy. But as the law stands at the moment there is nothing you can legally do to prevent their depredations. If you do take the law into your own hands and harm harriers, eggs or chicks, you are likely to find yourself being dealt with by the courts, and dealt with far more severely than if you had simply assaulted an old lady and stolen her handbag or driven away a few cars for joyriding and subsequent incineration. Like crows and magpies, however, foxes are still fair game, and provided you confine your activities to legal methods, they can still be discouraged from eating your game birds and their offspring.

In the case of the fox, legal methods can be split into two categories. There are the direct methods such as shooting, snaring and trapping, and the indirect methods which aim to keep the fox away from the more sensitive areas of the shoot by the use of electric fences and the like. Most shoots will not confine themselves to one or the other, but will endeavour to kill what foxes they can while keeping those that survive away from their poults, chicks and nesting hens.

The most common indirect method of fox control is the electric fence. A couple of strands of electrified wire strung around the outside of the release pen will discourage most foxes from even attempting to gain entry, and a good sting on the nose may put a fox off the scent of pheasant poult for life. The normal siting for an electric fence is around the perimeter of the release pen, although there is some evidence that it is just as effective even if it is well away from the actual perimeter. However, batteries can go flat, farm stock can blunder into the fence and break the wire, a blade of grass or bracken may short out a section of the fence, or you may just be unlucky enough to be host to a very thick-skinned fox. So although electric fences are a valuable tool in the battle against foxes, like all mechanical devices they are fallible and should never be your only means of defence.

Other devices which may deter foxes are transistor radios left to play near the pen, flashing lamps, various proprietary chemicals which smell revolting, at least to the fox, rags soaked in diesel oil, and strings of bird-scaring fireworks. However, most of these will also draw the attention of human predators to your release pen and so may prove more of a liability than an asset, although this will depend on the actual location of your shoot and the relations you have with the local community. The Game Conservancy is currently experimenting with ways of creating a vulpine aversion to game birds by enticing foxes to take a dead poult which has been laced with a foul-tasting ingredient. Some shoots, where the owner or the landlord is a hunting enthusiast, may even be expected to encourage foxes in limited numbers. For most shoots, however, the primary method of fox control is to reduce their numbers.

This is something of a labour of Hercules, since it is said, with some justification, that every time you kill one fox two others will come to the funeral. Some shoots kill fifty, sixty, seventy or more foxes every year, and yet there are never more than half a dozen resident on those shoots at any one time. Foxes are territorial, and a resident fox will prevent other foxes from invading its patch. Kill it, and another will soon move in. Even so, most shoots will practise some form of fox control, and for many keepers and shoot managers, lamping is almost a sport in its own right.

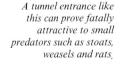

A tunnel entrance like this can prove fatally attractive to small predators such as stoats, weasels and rats.

New laws passed, first by the Scottish Parliament and later by Westminster, have attempted to ban what they describe as 'hunting with dogs'. Both sets of laws are inconsistent and muddled in their aims, and at the time of writing it is still unclear what exactly may or may not be legally permitted when using hounds to control foxes. Naturally, the law as passed by the Scottish Parliament differs from that passed by the Westminster MPs, so what is legal in Scotland may be illegal in England and Wales, but broadly the law allows huntsmen and keepers to use 'dogs' – hounds and terriers – to flush foxes in order that they may be shot. The law makes an exception for those occasions when the fox is caught and killed **before** it can be shot, provided that there was a real intention to shoot it. A keeper waiting with a loaded shotgun at the mouth of the den for his terrier to bolt a fox is clearly intent on killing it by shooting it. A marksman smoking a cigarette with his gun in a slip while hounds rattle through the covert, flush a fox and give chase may not be deemed to be making maximum effort to ensure a clean kill.

Flushing foxes to be run down by lurchers is no longer permissible, nor is using a terrier **deliberately** to kill cubs underground. The terrier must understand the need to flush them rather than kill them – or so our political masters have deemed. If you are shooting foxes a shotgun loaded with heavy shot – BBs or AAAs – should ensure that the bolting fox is killed quickly and cleanly if at all possible. If there is more than one gun waiting at the entrance to the den it is advisable to ensure that all are safe and experienced shots. A bolting fox can move very quickly indeed, and trying to loose off a couple of rounds of heavy shot with other people in close proximity is no task for a novice.

Lamping, using a high-powered spotlight and a rifle, accounts for many foxes every year. The technique is simple enough. You drive or walk around your patch after dark, shining your spotlight across the fields or moorland and watching for the tell-tale red glint of a fox's eyes. Then you unlimber the rifle and shoot it. Sometimes it can be just as easy as that. At other times it requires a little more experience and ingenuity. For a start, you need to be able to distinguish between the eyes of a fox and those of anything else which might be wandering about the fields. It is the glint of the light reflected in the animal's eyes that will catch your attention, and after a time you should be able to identify the owner of the eyes fairly easily using a combination of the colour reflected back to you and the way in which the eyes move around. It hardly needs to be said that you should never, under any circumstances, shoot until you are absolutely certain that your target is a fox. Certainty in identification comes with practice, and the best way to practise is to get out and about with a lamp. Take the rifle, but do not use it unless you have positively identified your target as a fox.

Some of today's spotlamps are extremely powerful, and can pick out the eyes of a fox at distances well beyond the ability of the average rifleman to kill it. This is where a useful trick called 'squeaking' comes into play. If you make a high-pitched squeaking or squealing sound in imitation of an injured rabbit, the fox is quite likely to trot up to investigate the possibilities of an easy meal. Some foxes will come to a squeak even though it means trotting along the beam of the spotlight. You can produce this squeak by moistening the back of your hand and then sucking it, by rubbing a piece of expanded polystyrene on the windscreen of your vehicle, or by using a proprietary fox-calling device.

Squeaking is also a useful way of luring foxes out from the cover of woods or under-growth. If you can master the technique – and some people seem to have an almost instinctive empathy with foxes – then it can work like a charm. If you are lamping on foot, using a battery-powered lamp, then the wind direction will be vital if you are to bring a fox in close enough for a shot. If the wind is blowing from you to the fox the chances of drawing it into range are much slimmer than if the wind is carrying your scent away from your intended victim. If you are in a vehicle scent seems to matter considerably less, possibly because of the combination of other smells – oil, fuel, exhaust fumes and the like – or perhaps because the fox is less inclined to associate the scent of a human in a vehicle with clear and present danger.

All that is required is to position yourself at a convenient distance from the wood, have a preliminary look around with the lamp and then give a few squeaks. Give the fox time to come and investigate, then have another cast about with the lamp. An experienced caller, on a good night, may bring a whole family of foxes out. It only takes a tiny squeak to attract a fox if it is there to be attracted. It may sound to your ears as though the sound will not carry more than a few feet, but I have seen a fox stop dead in its tracks in response to a tiny squeak, and that from a distance of at least 300 yards.

Strangely, a rifle shot, which echoes off the hills for miles in every direction, may not prevent other foxes from coming along to see what has happened to the first. I have seen the same thing when roe stalking. Step on a twig and every roe in the wood will be up on its feet and barking suspiciously as it bounds away, yet on more than one occasion I have seen an adult roe – not a calf looking for its mother, nor a mother seeking a calf, but a fully grown adult – come trotting up towards the sound of a shot. So if you draw one fox to a squeak it is always worth waiting a few minutes after you shoot it to see whether another comes along to investigate.

But beware of taking a speculative shot. Aside from the danger of wounding the animal, it is likely that a fox which has once been lured to a lamp only to have a hundred grains of copper-jacketed lead go whistling past his ears will never stand still in a spotlight again. Make sure of your target before thinking about a shot, then try and be certain

Fox drives at the end of the season will help to keep one of the worst predators of game birds in check.

of your shot before taking it. Perhaps most importantly of all, make sure that you know your ground intimately before even considering a lamping trip. A shot which misses and makes a fox lamp-shy is a nuisance. A shot which misses the fox but goes on to hit a house, a car, a farm animal or a person is going to mean the end of your firearms certificate, and quite possibly the end of your job and your liberty for a considerable spell. You should know what is behind your target and be quite sure that it is safe before firing.

Finally, it is wise to notify the police when you will be out with the lamp, particularly if your shoot is in a populated area, and to have a word with any residents on the shoot who might otherwise be disturbed by the crack of a fox rifle in the middle of the night.

Lamping is effective, and has the additional attraction of serving as a very visible deterrent to poachers. However, the lamp and the rifle are only effective when you are there behind them. Traps and snares can work for twenty-four hours a day and take up a lot less of your time, provided that you think ahead when setting out your trap line. You must, by law, inspect your snares and traps at least once a day; if this is not practical then do not set them unless you can arrange for someone else to inspect them in your absence. If your spare time is precious you should try and set out your traps so that you can get around them in the time you have available. The fox is mainly nocturnal, so the best time to go round your traps is the early morning, both to minimise any suffering on the part of the victim and to lessen the chance of a member of the public being outraged at the sight of a snared or trapped animal. It may mean crawling out of bed an hour or two earlier than you would choose, but your efforts should be rewarded in the shooting season.

The snare is the main weapon in the keeper's armoury when it comes to fox control. A fox wire must be free-running – self-locking snares which tighten round the victim's neck and will then not loosen off are illegal – and should have a twist of wire to act as a stop so that the snare will not close completely if it traps the leg of a deer, sheep, cow or something else you would prefer not to catch. You can fix the snare to a fence post, or to a stake driven very firmly into the ground, or alternatively you can tie it to a log or a spare fence post left lying on the ground. When the fox is caught it will be free to drag the post a few yards until it becomes tangled in trees or bushes. In theory this will stop a good catching place being spoiled as the victim claws up the ground while trying to escape, and it will prevent a snared fox from exerting its full strength against a fixed object and possibly breaking the wire.

Set your snare across a known fox run, or near a gap in a fence where the fox squeezes through. Be sure that it *is* a fox run: look for footprints in soft mud, fox droppings, sandy-reddish fur snagged on fences and any other clues to the user of the run. You do not want to end up with a roe deer or a badger in your snare instead of a fox, nor indeed somebody's pet dog or cat. Setting the snare in a gap under a fence is dangerous as it will catch any animal which squeezes through that gap, including badgers and deer. Where a fox is believed to be using a gap under a fence set your snare a few yards back from the fence and try to catch him as he approaches or leaves the gap rather than as he is actually squeezing through it.

If set in the open at the proper height above the ground, a fox wire is far less likely to catch a badger, which will probably have its nose below the bottom of the wire, or a roe deer, which will step over it. You can encourage the deer to go over the snare by arranging a branch above the wire that will invite deer to jump but foxes to slip underneath. The snare should be set in a loop about 9 inches wide by about 6 inches deep, with the lower edge of the loop held about 6 inches off the ground by a tealer – a short stick split open at one end to grip the wire and sharpened at the other to push into the ground.

Snares can also be set in sensitive areas such as the borders of rearing fields and release pens, even if there are no obvious signs of fox runs. This is a pre-emptive measure, and has a better chance of succeeding if you set the snare somewhere where the access narrows and would tend to edge a passing fox towards the wire. If no such spot occurs naturally you may be able to create one with a little judicious placing of logs, straw bales, brush-wood or the like. This is what might be termed a speculative use of snares – setting them in a vulnerable spot in the hope of catching a fox if one should happen by, as opposed to the more specific method of setting them to target a known fox run.

There is a third strategy which you might like to consider, where snares are set in a par-ticular spot to which you hope to lure any local foxes. This is what is sometimes known as a midden trap. The principle used to be simple. Foxes are clever and efficient hunters if need be, but they are also quite happy to eat carrion if it is available. This can be turned to your advantage by placing some kind of bait where the foxes should find it, and sur-rounding it with snares. The usual method was to half bury a sheep carcass, or anything similar that was handy, and set snares around it. If a damp, rushy spot was chosen the burying was easy and 'runs' could be trampled through the rushes in which the snares were set. Alternatively, the carcass could be surrounded by a circle of sheep netting to keep stock and domestic dogs away from it and the snares. One strand of wire could then be cut to allow easy entry for the fox and the snare would be set just inside the netting. The scent of the bait and the prospect of a free lunch lured the foxes, and if one fox was snared there was a fair chance that others might come along to see what the fuss was about and perhaps get snared as well.

A centre-fire rifle equipped with a good telescopic sight is the ideal weapon for fox control when lamping.

Midden traps were a useful weapon in the keeper's armoury, but since the foot and mouth outbreak in 2001 (when the Government ordered the slaughter and burial of several million sheep and cattle) it is illegal to bury farm animal carcasses. Preparing a midden trap with a dead sheep or calf might lead to you making an appearance before the local magistrates. But you might like to try an alternative bait. Foxes are supposed to be fond of the smellier varieties of cat food, and a few tins emptied out and heeled into the ground in the centre of your circle of snares might be even more effective than a dead lamb.

Small Ground Predators

The main small ground predators are the stoat, the weasel, the rat and the mink. The first three are commonly taken by tunnel traps, whereas the mink is usually caught in a cage trap. There are body-grip traps which are approved for use against mink but great care is needed if you are not to catch otters in the same traps. A cage trap is just as effective, and allows you to release any creature that is caught by mistake.

Cage traps can be bought ready to use, or made up at home. The principle is simple: a wire cage is equipped with a spring-loaded door which will slam shut when a trigger is released. The trigger is activated by the weight of the animal on a plate at the end of the cage furthest from the entrance and the mink can be encouraged to enter the cage by the use of a bait such as fish, rabbit or cat food. Indeed, it has a lively curiosity and may find its way into the trap simply because it is there. Mink are generally found near water, along river banks and streams and beside ponds and lakes. You can disguise your trap by placing it in a hole in the bank or an artificial tunnel in order to play on the animal's curiosity and, incidentally, to keep the trap out of the sight of passing hikers. The Game Conservancy catch mink on 'mink islands' – small rafts floating offshore with a cage trap set ready for the mink that hauls itself out of the water to investigate the smell of the bait.

Once you have a lively mink in your cage you will need the means to dispose of it humanely. A mink has very sharp teeth set in strong jaws, and if trapped it will have no hesitation in sinking them into any part of you that is available. So take a gun, a .22 rifle or a powerful air rifle, with you when you inspect your traps and shoot your captive *in situ*, taking care not to damage the cage. A strong pair of leather gloves might also prove useful if you catch an otter by mistake and need to handle the cage in order to release it alive.

A tunnel trap is exactly what the name implies: a body-grip trap set inside some form of tunnel, which can be made from three boards nailed together, a length of pipe, bricks or from whatever natural materials are to hand. You can dig a trench and cover it with a board or a flat rock, make a small cairn of stones with the trap in the centre or use a natural tunnel such as a dry drainage pipe. The trap is set in the middle of the tunnel if it is open at both ends, or far enough in to be out of sight from outside if it is entered from one end only.

Tunnels should be sited in places where a passing stoat or weasel is likely to find them and feel impelled to inspect their interiors. You can leave some bait such as rabbit liver in the tunnel to act as an inducement, but often the very sight of a dark hole just waiting to be explored is enough to lure the victims to their deaths. Obvious sites for traps are around the edges of your rearing and release pens, where predators will be attracted by the scent and sound of your game birds, and around your feed stores, where rats will congregate. Out on the shoot, these small predators tend to travel along hedge lines and stone walls, and these are the places to target. A tunnel can be made even more inviting by creating an artificial run leading to the entrance. This should guide any passing predator towards the opening, at which point curiosity and the smell of the bait should lure it inside.

Traps will catch both predators and other species which you would not wish to harm, however, so you must try to ensure that pheasant poults, hedgehogs and other animals do not end up in them instead of the intended victims. Two sticks pushed firmly into the ground at the tunnel entrance will allow stoats, weasels or rats to squeeze in while hopefully excluding pheasants and any passing hedgehogs, rabbits or squirrels.

Rats can be caught in tunnel traps, but if you have a real problem with them, or with mice, you will almost certainly need to revert to the use of poison. An anticoagulant poison such as Warfarin can be set for rats provided that it is placed in such a way that it is not available to other animals – including your gundogs and farm stock. An agricultural merchant can supply you with it ready mixed with bait, or you can mix it up yourself. Place the poisoned bait where the rats will find it, underneath buildings such as chicken huts, below sheets of tin, in the back of a wood shed or in wooden boxes made for the purpose. These poisons work on a cumulative basis, so you must set them and then keep replenishing them until the rats and mice are no longer eating them – hopefully because they are all dead. You may decide to establish baiting points as a preventative measure even though there are no current signs of rat and mouse damage. Regular inspection will soon show you if anything is starting to take the bait and potential problems may thus be prevented before there is any real damage to the shoot. If you do this it is particularly important that your baiting points are, and will remain, secure from other animals, as the poisoned bait is likely to be around for a considerable time.

Predator control is an emotive issue and raises strong feelings among those whose job it is to raise game and keep it free from predation and those who object to the culling of predators. It is noticeable that objections are generally limited to the more 'cuddly' predators and often have geographical restrictions. One rarely hears of animal rights activists defending the rights of rats for example, and a fox which moves into town and starts raiding dustbins will get a much less sympathetic reception than one which is raiding my release pen. Those organisations which rear fox cubs and then release them into the wild invariably release them well away from their own backyards. Incidentally, such releases strike me as cruel as well as futile. A hand-reared fox has little chance of surviving in the wild. If you reared a litter of puppies and then dumped them out to fend for themselves you would, quite properly, be accused of acting in a cruel and callous manner. Why should a fox cub be regarded any differently?

Double standards seem to be prevalent among many of those who would take away my right to protect my property – especially when that property takes the form of a pheasant, grouse or partridge. For example, an eagle in the countryside must be allowed to do whatever it likes with no interference from man, but I wonder what would happen if a pair of eagles moved into a town, nested on the side of a tower block and began to feed on pet cats, small dogs and the like? Would they still be sacrosanct? A rabbit in the countryside is a delightful, furry creature; a rabbit in a vegetable garden is an unmitigated pest. A fox killing my pheasant poults is only doing what comes naturally to a fox; the same fox raiding a hutch for a pet rabbit is a vicious killer.

The protection of certain predators has, in my opinion, gone beyond the bounds of common sense. Raptor populations did take a disastrous dive a few years ago because of the effects of DDT and Dieldrin, but they are now recovering, and in some cases recovering rapidly. There has to be a sense of proportion to the matter of predator control. I am not suggesting that any keeper should be allowed to shoot and trap predators just as the fancy takes him, but there should certainly be procedures available to protect game birds, lambs and other stock from excessive predation when it occurs. If it can be shown that the attention of a particular predator, or group of predators, is threatening the economic survival of, for example, an area of moorland, then it should be possible to take steps to bring the matter under control – under licence certainly, but with at least some chance of obtaining such a licence.

However, I see little prospect of any such legislation being introduced in the near future. Indeed, I think it likely that any changes in the law are likely to be more restrictive rather than less. The law may be all kinds of an ass, but in the end it *is* the law, and it is incumbent upon us all to obey it – no matter how ridiculous it may be.

8 Habitat Improvement

There are a lot of ways in which you can make your shoot a better place for the game which lives there. Some are simple to conceive, easy to execute and cost practically nothing; others might involve a great deal of effort and require sums of money that would make a billionnaire blanch. In many cases there will be grants and subsidies available to help finance a project, although usually these official sources of funding are not primarily intended to subsidise the shooting community. Nevertheless, if the government is willing to pay you to plant a wood, and if by doing so you can improve the prospects for your pheasants, I can see no reason not to take advantage of the cash on offer. Indeed, even if you do not want the grants and the subsidies, you will still have to put up with a certain amount of official meddling in the form of planning permissions and the like before you will be allowed to do as you wish on your own land.

Improving the habitat for game usually means providing food, shelter and protection from predators. All game, be it feathered, furred or finned, has three main requirements from life. It needs a safe place to live, a regular supply of food and the chance to reproduce. If you can improve the supply of some or all of the above then you and your shoot should benefit. A great deal of other wildlife will probably also enjoy the results of your efforts, and I am not simply referring to the predators which will come along to eat the

Heather-burning is the basis of good grouse-moor management.

extra game which you hope to encourage. When you plant a wood or dig a pond, establish a hedgerow or thin out an overgrown plantation to let in the sunlight and encourage plant growth you create a new habitat that will become home to a whole ecosystem of plants, insects, birds and mammals as well as the pheasants, ducks, trout, deer, or other species that were your intended beneficiaries. In many cases it will be by encouraging insects and weeds to grow in odd corners of the shoot that you will be able to improve the habitat for your game birds which rely on them for food and shelter.

Interfering with the environment is a potentially dangerous activity, and may produce hidden results that will, in the long term, more than offset any short term benefits that may accrue. Consider modern organophosphate pesticides. In order to produce ever larger mountains of unwanted foodstuffs the farming industry was encouraged to destroy vital links in the food chain. Kill off all the insects and you decimate all the birds which rely on those insects to feed themselves and their young. Grub out the hedgerows and fill in the ponds and the ditches and you take away their nesting sites. Higher up the food chain the cumulative effect of the chemicals reduces the shell thickness of the eggs of birds of prey and a disastrous decline in breeding success almost wipes out harriers, peregrines, buzzards, eagles and the like. The agrichemical industry may have made a lot of people very wealthy, but it has been at an enormous, and a not yet fully understood, cost. We are part of that food chain too, and we breathe the air which has been polluted by those poisonous sprays and eat the food which has been coated with them. There may be further effects to come which we have not seen as yet.

Having said that, there is some environmental meddling that we, as shooting enthusiasts, might feel justified in undertaking. Here the picture is somewhat brighter, and you can set about practically any of the accepted ways of improving the habitat on your shoot with a clear conscience. What is good for pheasants, partridges, grouse and wildfowl is almost invariably good for the rest of the ecosystem of which they are a part. One possible exception might be heather burning, where the smoke adds to the pollution of the atmosphere, but at least it is clean smoke, unadulterated with acids, heavy metals and all the other delights that industrial chimneys pump into our skies.

The extent to which you will be able to improve your shoot will depend on a number of factors. The first thing to ascertain is exactly what you are allowed to do. If you are a shooting tenant the terms of your lease may limit your actions, as will the requirements of any other legitimate users of the land. If you happen to be both farmer and shoot manager there may be no problem if, wearing your shoot manager's hat, you decide to establish three or four new 10-acre woodlands on part of the arable acreage, or to double the area devoted to game crop. If you are just a shooting tenant, however, you will certainly need to clear any such changes with both the landlord and the farmer.

Equally, even if there is agreement between all parties regarding the changes you would like to make, there may still be problems to be encountered from officialdom. You may need planning permission. The ground may be part of an SSSI (Site of Special Scientific Interest) or an ESS (Environmental Stewardship Scheme) which replaced the old ESA (Environmentally Sensitive Area) designation. If so, you will need to agree any actions with the appropriate authorities before you make a start. This is often not as painful as it sounds. Given the right approach and a sensible plan, you will probably get a great deal of co-operation and help, both physical and financial, from the various agencies involved. Of course you may not, but you must still follow the correct procedures or you may end up having to spend a great deal more money to restore things to the way they were before you 'improved' them.

Before setting out with the chainsaw or planting spade you might like to give some thought to the adage 'If it ain't broke, don't mend it.' A new wood on flat ground below an old slate quarry *might* be excellent for holding pheasants, but would it be an improvement if it attracted all the birds down from a hanging wood at the top of a nearby hill and thus ruined your best drive? Planting a mass of shrubs below the trees in a wood *might* improve the cover for the pheasants, but would it improve the shooting if the beaters were then unable to flush them? A shelter belt right at the top of a hill *might* form the basis of a really exciting drive, but only if you could persuade the birds to stay there, and only if you could get up there yourself to feed them once the ground was too wet for a vehicle to make the trip.

I am not suggesting that you should never try to improve the quality of your shoot. However, I do suggest that you take stock of what you have before starting out on any project that may eventually prove expensive, might have a deleterious effect on your sport rather than enhancing it, and might be irreversible once it has been done. That said, most shoot managers will quickly be able to think of any number of projects, both large and small, that would benefit the shoot: a new cover strip here, a bit more bottom in a particular wood, a wet corner that could be dredged out to provide a flight pond, or a dozen other ideas.

New Woodlands

Mixed, open woodland like this is ideal for woodcock.

If you are running an ordinary driven pheasant type of shoot then the odds are that some, if not all, of your drives will involve flushing pheasants out of one piece of woodland and flying them across to another. The woods – or more correctly, the woodland margins – are

home for the pheasants: they feed there, sleep there, nest there and live most of their lives in and around them. It follows, therefore, that one obvious way to improve your shoot is by adding new woodlands or by improving the quality of those that are already in place.

Establishing a new wood is an expensive project, and one which will be with you for many years to come. As far as the expense goes, there are a number of schemes designed to assist landowners with the creation, maintenance and improvement of woodland. The scope of these schemes and the size of the payments vary, so there is little point in quoting specific figures here. The local office of the Department for the Environment, Food and Rural Affairs (England and Wales) or the Scottish Executive Environment and Rural Affairs Department will be able to supply you with the latest details, plus application forms and advice on how to proceed. Money may be available for the management of established woodlands as well as for the creation of new ones, and grants can currently be obtained for natural regeneration as well as for actually planting trees. If you are considering any sort of woodland scheme it is well worth discussing the matter with your local DEFRA or SEERAD office, if only to prevent you from doing something that may not be permitted under the maze of regulations which are apparently vital to managing the countryside and keeping lots of civil servants in well-paid employment.

Very briefly, one or more of the following schemes may be of interest to you if you are embarking on a woodland project. The list is not comprehensive; in particular there are many individual schemes run by local authorities, national parks and the like which may be available in your particular area.

• **Energy Crops Scheme:** Provides grants to set up coppice woodlands intended to provide renewable/sustainable fuel supplies, but likely to make ideal pheasant coverts.

Grants are available for natural regeneration as well as for planting trees.

• **English Woodland Grant Scheme:** Grants to private landowners to encourage the creation of new woodlands and to assist with the management of existing woodlands. In a similar vein are the:

• **Scottish Forestry Grants Scheme:** And the:

• **Woodland Grants Scheme:** With transitional arrangements to:

• **Better Woodlands for Wales:** All of which are similar to the English Woodland Grant Scheme in that they provide assistance for the provision of new and the management of existing woods. In addition there may be additional grants available for planting trees on farmland via Woodlands in England, the Farm Woodlands Premium Scheme (in Wales) or the Scottish Forestry Grants Scheme: Farmlands Premium.

• **Environmental Stewardship Scheme:** Follows on from the now discontinued Environmentally Sensitive Areas Scheme and the Countryside Stewardship Scheme with the stated objectives of:

  Conserving wildlife,
  Maintaining and enhancing the quality and character of the landscape,
  Protecting the historic environment and natural resources, and
  Promoting public access and understanding of the countryside.

• **Local Heritage Initiative:** Which provides grants for local groups to investigate, explain and care for their local landscape, landmarks, traditions and culture.

• **Rural Enterprise Scheme:** Which supports projects aiming to develop more sustainable, diversified and enterprising rural economies and communities.

• **Wildspace Grant Scheme:** Which provides grants to local communities for Local Nature Reserves.

• **Land Purchase Grants:** English Nature grants to voluntary nature conservation organisations to acquire and manage important areas of land, and the:

• **Vocational Training Scheme:** That funds vocational training for those engaged in farming or forestry.

There are other grants and incentives, and changes are made to the existing schemes on a regular basis. The most important thing to remember if you are looking for grant aid with any woodland scheme is to get in touch with the correct authorities before you start work, or even before you finalise your plans. Many of the payments are available only if your scheme matches all the requirements of the granting body, and in most cases no money will be paid if you start work before agreeing your plans with those authorities. Also, in many cases the grants might not be available to you as a shooting tenant, although they would be available to the landlord or perhaps the farming tenant. Check this well in advance as you may need to channel any grant applications through them rather than making an application on your own behalf.

But what should you do, whether you are being assisted by public money or meeting the full cost from your own pockets? If your intention is to plant a completely new wood you will naturally give a great deal of thought to where it should be sited. The layout of your shoot or the requirements of the farming enterprise may dictate this to the extent that there is little or no choice, but if you do have a number of possible sites in view you might be best to carry out a few experiments before making the final decision. Once the trees have been planted they are there for a long, long time, so, if you are uncertain about how well a particular drive might work if a new wood is established in a particular place, you may be able to put in a game crop for one or two seasons and see whether the birds will fly as well as you hope from there. This will add a little extra cost, of course, as well as delaying the planting of the new wood, but both the expense and the delay will be well justified if it turns out that your initial choice of site was not such a good idea after all. Obviously, if you have a number of possible sites in mind you can extend this idea further and plant several blocks of game crop.

The layout of the wood may be dictated by the ground available for planting, or by what the landlord or farmer is prepared to allow. If you do have a choice of shape, however, it is worth remembering that a long, narrow wood will be easier for the beaters to work than a big square area. Also, as the pheasant is a bird of the woodland margins, it is better to maximise the length of the edges rather than the acreage of the wood.

The type of trees you plant will be dictated to a large extent by where your shoot is, by the type of soil you have and by the normal weather conditions in your part of the country. The various grant- and subsidy-providing bodies will also want to have a say in what goes in, as will the landlord and the farmer. As far as the shoot is concerned, you may want quick-growing trees such as conifers to enable the wood to come into use as soon as possible, or you may prefer hardwoods such as beech and oak which will eventually be more attractive to the pheasants as providers of acorns and beech mast. In practice, a mixture of hardwoods and softwoods is likely to be the best solution, perhaps with some game crop sown around the margins, or even in clearings among the trees, to encourage pheasants to hold there while the young trees are becoming established.

One of the most expensive aspects of creating a wood can be the cost of keeping rabbits, hares and deer away from your young trees. Stock fencing will almost certainly be needed to keep sheep and cattle out, but a normal stock fence will not even slow down these wild animals. Fencing the whole wood with rabbit netting is an expensive option, but one that may be necessary if your soil conditions and local rabbit population demand it. A better alternative, in certain cases, are individual plastic tree protectors which can be fitted over every sapling, as these will not only keep deer and rabbits away from the trees but will also provide a microclimate which should speed the trees' growth. In addition, a wood which is impervious to rabbits is also very difficult for pheasants to use, as they would much rather walk to where they are going than fly there. The fencing can also be a nuisance when beating the wood, as the pheasants have a tendency to become trapped against it and then pegged by an over-eager gundog.

Existing Woodlands

While planting a complete new wood might not be practical or financially viable on your shoot, it is probable that you will be able to improve the game-holding potential of the woods which are already there. The first thing to do is to take stock of what you have and, if you have been shooting the ground already, how well it works at the moment. Again, bear in mind the maxim 'If it ain't broke, don't mend it' and be very wary of making any major changes to a wood which already holds birds and lends itself to presenting them well over the guns. Change is not always synonymous with improvement, and it is quite possible to ruin a good drive by 'improving' it.

The objective of shoot woodland management is to produce coverts that will hold game – perhaps just in the shooting season, or possibly right through the year if you have a stock of wild birds which breed on the shoot. In theory it is possible to specify the type of woodland that will attract pheasants or woodcock, although in practice the birds can sometimes confound this accepted wisdom. Dark, gloomy fir plantations and cold, bare beech woods are all supposed to be poor for game holding, and they generally are, but there are occasional exceptions. Pheasants can be stubborn little brutes at times, and if they insist on making their home in a thick stand of Sitka spruce, then you might as well accept it, provide them with some feeders and work our the best way to get them over the guns.

Generally, however, if you have a wood containing a variety of timber, with some dense undergrowth to give the birds cover and some open spaces where they can sun themselves and dry out after rain, if there are suitable roosting trees – perhaps some with ivy for warmth on winter nights – and some oak and beech to provide natural food, if the wood is not regularly disturbed by dogs or hikers, and if a good hedge breaks the wind so that the birds are not frozen on windy winter days, then you probably have a wood which will hold game. It follows then that any improvements that you make to the existing woods should aim to produce any of these conditions that are currently lacking.

Cutting back trees where they are too dense may not be permitted under your shooting tenancy, although this will probably depend on the value of the timber which you propose felling. Clearing out some scrub is unlikely to cause any friction with the owner, but felling an acre or two of mature oaks might be less acceptable. If you think ahead before you start with the chainsaw you may be able to let quite a lot of light into the gloomier areas of the wood with only minimal damage to standing timber.

Planting shrubs and bushes to give ground cover for your birds is less likely to cause problems, but you should beware of introducing species which may eventually run riot and spoil the wood for future generations if not for your own shoot. Obviously, you should choose ground-cover plants, shrubs and bushes that are suitable for the area and the soil on your shoot. If the lack of ground cover is due to a lack of light it may be necessary to combine your planting programme with some judicious pruning. Indeed, if a lack of light is the major problem then remedying this may be all that is required. Once some sunshine is let through to the woodland floor the ground cover may regenerate naturally.

Cover can also be produced by trimming some of the lower branches and leaving heaps of the brashings on the ground for the birds to squat under. The trimming may be required in any case to make rides for the beaters, or to let light into the wood, so you can sometimes kill two birds with the one stone and produce instant cover with the brashings while encouraging regrowth to give cover in future seasons.

If a wood is cold and draughty because it is in an exposed position the solution may lie outside the wood itself. Planting a hedge or arranging some other form of windbreak along the side where the prevailing wind strikes can dramatically improve the wood's game-holding capacity. Planting a hedge is undoubtedly the most environmentally correct procedure, but it will be several years before any benefits are seen. In the short term you could consider running a strip of plastic windbreak netting along the woodland edge, or persuading the farmer to store a line of big bales there if the wood is not too remote from where the straw or silage will be needed eventually.

The problem may also be an excess of cover rather than a lack of it. If the cover is too dense or too extensive it can be very difficult for the beaters and dogs to find and flush the game. A pheasant can sit surprisingly tightly, particularly towards the end of the season when it has learned what taking flight will entail as it crosses the line of guns. Hacking and slashing rides through the undergrowth is hard, hot work but can be well worth the effort when shooting begins.

Heather moorland on the left of the fence, grass on the right – the result of liming and reseeding.

Game Cover Crops

Game cover crops are being used more and more to provide 'instant' pheasant coverts, to increase the scope of a shoot without the expense of creating new woodlands, to provide a means of holding pheasants throughout the season and to provide an additional food source for the birds. The mixtures and varieties which can be obtained now, either as ready-mixed game crop sowings or made up to your own specification, are legion. The right choice for your shoot will depend to a very large extent on where you are located, as a crop which might be ideal on the chalk downlands of southern England would be unlikely to thrive in the acid peat of Caithness.

Game crop can be used simply as holding cover on shoots where the fields and woods tend to become bare by mid-season, or it can be grown primarily as a food crop using plants such as sunflowers, maize, beans, oats, millet and suchlike. Kale, canary grass, root crops such as fodder beet and turnips, artichokes or rape will provide cover, although not much in the way of food, and in general, game crops tend to be a mixture of food plants and cover plants. Some crops need to be replanted every spring, while others can be left to reseed themselves over a number of years.

The place to plant your game crop is obviously where you want your birds to be when you are organising your drives. The crop is often grown along the edges of a wood, the

Odd corners which can be left to grow wild will quickly provide valuable game cover.

idea being to offer an alternative and attractive habitat for the birds close by their normal roosting and feeding area. This is one way of hedging your bets for a shoot day, as with two different habitats close together you would hope to find the birds in one or the other, whatever the weather.

Game crop is also commonly used to create a completely new drive, where there is a shortage of suitable woodland or where extra drives are required on the shoot. The balance between the need for food and the need for cover will vary according to where the crop is planted, although it is worth remembering that feeders can be placed in a strip of crop that has cover but little food value. If the crop offers food but little shelter it is unlikely to attract birds in the depths of winter, and will in any case be difficult to show birds from once they have gained an understanding of the implications of a shooting day. Birds which feel too exposed will take to their wings – or more likely to their legs – as soon as the beaters hove into view.

The headlands of arable fields are good sites for game crop, particularly if there is a decent hedge to provide shelter from the weather and a natural lead into the crop for wandering poults. Under the set-aside rules (of which more in a moment) it may be possible to establish strips of game cover as part of the set-aside acreage for the farm. This use of field margins will also benefit many other forms of wildlife as well as producing useful nesting cover for your wild birds in the spring, provided that an appropriate mixture is selected for the game crop.

Advice on the best mixtures to grow locally can be obtained from the Game Conservancy or from a local seed merchant, provided that he has a good appreciation of the needs of the shoot. When planting crop it is better to err on the generous side, since tiny patches of game crop may hold the odd bird but are unlikely to attract enough to make any sort of drive. The farmer or farm tenant is, not unnaturally, entitled to expect some compensation for any land taken out of production in order to establish game crops, and this should reflect a fair return compared with what the land would have made if it had been left to grow grass or cereals.

Conservation Headlands

I believe the term 'conservation headland' was coined by the Game Conservancy. I am borrowing it here because I can think of no better way to describe the use of field margins to produce areas of cover and food for game and other birds. Insects, insect larvae, weed seeds and wild plants all form important links in the food chain for many wild birds apart from pheasants and partridges, and it is around the edges of fields and in hedgerows that many of these birds nest and raise their young. Leaving a narrow strip uncultivated along the side of the hedge and then keeping insecticide and herbicide sprays off the outer strip of the main field crop will have little effect on farm production, but it can be of enormous benefit to the partridges, skylarks, curlews and other ground-nesting birds which rely on a ready supply of insects and weed seeds to raise their young.

All that is needed is for the headlands to be left when the sprayer is covering the remainder of the crop. The insects that flourish in the unsprayed strip will provide your partridges with the high-protein diet that they must feed their chicks in the first fortnight after they hatch, and the weeds and wild flowers will help to feed the adults and to encourage the insects. You may also be able to persuade the farmer to consider using part of the field margin as set-aside acreage if he is taking advantage of the set-aside scheme.

This strip left to grow under the hawthorns will provide nesting sites and cover for game birds.

Set-aside

As with the grants and subsidies for woodland planting and regeneration, the rules concerning set-aside payments are both complicated and frequently amended. The principle seems simple enough. Because European Union farmers are producing more grain, wine, milk, butter, olives, beef, mutton and so on than we can possibly eat, the people in Brussels will pay them lots of money – your money and my money – not to produce that grain, grapes, milk, butter and meat. In theory, all that happens is that a farmer reduces the

Leaving uncut headlands in silage fields will benefit game birds at very little cost.

acreage under cultivation by an agreed amount and receives compensation in return. In practice, the men from the ministries have got involved and written some rules and guidelines, and in consequence there is now a whole army of civil servants being paid a great deal of money to supervise farmers not growing anything.

'Not growing anything' is not quite the whole story, however. Land which is designated for set-aside can be planted with certain non-commercial mixtures of crops, some of which are excellent game cover for nesting or for holding birds during the shooting season. Even if the land is simply left fallow the subsequent growth of weeds and wild flowers can make useful nesting cover, although under the regulations it will have to be mowed or sprayed during the summer – hopefully after the ground-nesting birds have removed their broods.

Because the rules and regulations for set-aside change frequently there is little point in being too specific. One point that must be remembered is that a farmer may not accept set-aside payments while putting the land to an alternative commercial use. For example, if set-aside land was rented out to motor-cycle enthusiasts for scramble riding the set-aside money would almost certainly be forfeited. However, if you would have shot over the land anyway even if it was in production, there is no reason why set-aside should not be planned with the maximum benefit to the shoot in mind – provided of course that your relationship with the farmer will lend itself to such an arrangement, and that your rent is not increased as a result.

Some set-aside can be planned in the form of new woodlands, which takes the land permanently out of production, while other acreages can be out of production only for a limited time. Strips of set-aside along field margins can be especially beneficial to game birds, providing nesting sites, shelter, food in the form of insects and weed seeds and, eventually, a strip of cover which can feed a drive. If you happen to be farmer as well as shoot manager you can organise your set-aside to maximise the benefits for both the shoot and the agricultural side of your business. If you have control only of the shooting then you must negotiate with the farmer to see to what extent he may be willing to modify his set-aside plans for your benefit.

Ponds and Wetlands

When I was growing up in Suffolk there were ponds all over the place: ponds in the corners of fields to water the stock, ponds in cottage gardens where the clay had been dug to make wattle and daub walls, horse ponds in every farmyard and ornamental ponds in front of many of the larger houses. Today little remains of many of those ponds beyond a damp spot in the middle of a prairie field where the corn grows a little greener during a summer

Beaters among birch scrub which has been encouraged to regenerate naturally.

drought. A number do remain, however, and if you have a pond or two on your shoot you should be able to attract duck for flight shooting.

If there is no suitable pond you may well be able to create one, possibly with very little difficulty, simply by blocking an outflow at a suitable spot in a ditch or by getting a digger in to deepen a wet spot. The best site from the point of view of creating a pool of water is likely to be in one of the places where an old pond was filled in, and clues to these spots can be found on old maps, or simply by looking at the lie of the land. Low spots where water congregates naturally after rain, damp and boggy field corners or places where ditches widen out are all likely pond sites.

As far as the shooting goes, the pond needs to be isolated, but not too isolated. It needs to be far enough away from roads and houses so that the ducks will be confident enough to flight in for their food without the constant disturbance of people, dogs or passing traffic, and it should be in a spot where you will be able to shoot during the early evening without disturbing the neighbours unduly. It should also be accessible, bearing in mind that when the flight is over you will have to return home in pitch darkness carrying your shooting gear plus whatever you have shot. A long walk out to the flight pond in the gathering dusk may be quite pleasant; the same walk back when you cannot see where you are going may prove quite different.

It does not take much of a pond to draw in ducks, provided that it is fed regularly, ideally with barley or chat potatoes. The aim should be to feed the pond every day, and to provide only the quantity of food that will be cleaned out in a single evening. The ducks should then flight in at dusk to eat their rations and not sit about the pond all day getting fat only to disappear when you turn up for evening flight. In practice you may not be able to get to the pond every day, in which case you will either have to put out enough food to last until your next visit or install some kind of automatic feeding device. This once- or twice-weekly food scattering routine will work – I do it myself on a pond which is well out on our hill shoot – but there will be considerable waste of food to other aquatic feeders who enjoy a free meal of barley, and a danger of the food running out between visits.

The size of the pond is not important. We have a tiny flight pond which is really no more than an occasionally wet spot in the corner of a meadow, but it draws duck every season, if it is fed regularly. Depth is important in that shallow margins which allow the ducks to dabble for their grain are necessary, ideally combined with some deeper parts where they will feel safe from foxes, and some gently sloping margins that they can waddle out on to preen. Very large ponds have the potential to attract very large numbers of ducks, but they can be difficult to shoot as the ducks can drop in out of range of the guns. If you plan to shoot the pond alone or with just one or two companions, a small pond is ideal, but if you want to use the duck flight as a final 'drive' for a full team of guns you will need a big one, or perhaps better, three or four small ones scattered about the shoot.

If you are creating a new pond you should aim to have a combination of shallows and deeper pools and ideally incorporate an island or two which may encourage the ducks to nest in the spring as well as providing a haven from foxes, cats and the like. You can provide cover by planting reeds and rushes in the shallows, but beware of overdoing this as they can multiply rapidly and will need cutting back every spring to prevent them taking over the whole pond – another reason for incorporating deeper pools which should remain as open water.

You should show considerable restraint when shooting a pond. If you shoot too heavily and too often you can quickly discourage the ducks from using it. More importantly, there are more and more flight ponds being brought into use now and excessive shooting could have a serious effect on the wild duck population. The occasional foray – perhaps once a fortnight at the most – combined with a sensible bag limit and an end to shooting while the ducks are still coming in will not overexploit the resource and should allow you to enjoy flighting right through the season. In particular, if you have a spring-fed pond which stays open when other ponds in the area are frozen, you should resist any temptation to take large numbers of ducks from it in hard weather.

Wetland habitats such as bogs, marshes, fens, water meadows and the like have disappeared at an alarming rate over the last few years. Draining and ditching has turned huge areas of wetland into productive arable land, although as we have seen, much of that productive land is now being taken out of production at our expense in order to reduce the mountains of various unwanted foodstuffs that our masters in Europe have created on our behalf. Although any farmer is likely to have a natural and sensible aversion to taking a well-drained field and returning it to a wet, rushy bog, it may be possible to take odd corners and low-lying strips which are too wet for normal arable production and allow them to revert to marshland.

The shoot may not derive any great benefit from this, apart from the occasional foray after snipe, but even a few wet corners can add a bit of variety to a day's shooting. I suspect that before too long there will be grants available for recreating wetlands and bogs, as there are now for regenerating heather and planting hedgerows, and we may then see some of the lost habitat being restored. It may not be good agricultural practice, but I for one would welcome it, even if the money for the grants was coming out of my taxes. There are plenty of far worse ways in which our 'obedient servants' squander their share of our earnings.

It is important to remember that non-toxic shot must be used when shooting over a flight pond. The law differs slightly in that Scotland has banned the use of lead shot when shooting over wetland while in England and Wales it is illegal to shoot wildfowl and waders with lead shot no matter where you are shooting. In either case, shooting a flight pond means that lead shot is banned and you must use steel or one of the other alternative materials.

(Opposite):
Even a tiny splash such as this will attract duck if it is fed regularly and not disturbed too often.

Farming Practice

It is sometimes possible to help the shoot along simply by varying the timings of some of the work around the farm. If stubbles can be left for a few weeks – or better still, months – after harvest your pheasants and partridges can benefit enormously. Silaging, which takes place a few weeks earlier than haymaking once did, may well be a major factor in the decline of ground-nesting birds and hares, which are then at their most vulnerable time with eggs or young concealed in the grass and unable to escape the blades of the modern forage harvester. While it is hardly possible to delay the first cut for silage it may be possible to alleviate some of the damage. If you can run a dog through the field immediately before cutting you may be able to shift some game to safer pastures. If the field is cut starting in the centre and working outwards it will encourage birds and mammals to move out to safety.

Anything which preserves cover for the game will be welcome. Odd corners left to grow wild, hedges which are not cut back to the bare bones every year, field margins left unsprayed and allowed to produce a crop of weeds and insects, ditches which are not converted into bare drains with a mechanical digger and ponds allowed to flourish naturally, will all improve the land for game and for other wildlife, and will ultimately add value to the farm. A viable shoot is an attractive inducement if a farm comes on to the market, as well as producing extra income in the form of a shooting lease while the farm is in hand.

It is an interesting thought that a great deal of time and money is being spent on research to establish the reasons for the decline of the partridge, the grouse and other wild birds. It is something of an oversimplification, but game did flourish under the farming methods which were practised fifty and 100 years ago, and would almost certainly flourish again if we returned to those methods. I appreciate that the likelihood of that happening while there are still reserves of fossil fuel is practically non-existent, but, almost any concession to those old methods will help a little.

Cutting stubbles a little higher to provide cover and then leaving them uncultivated through the autumn, managing hedgerows so that there is shelter and nesting cover for wild birds, trying to avoid nests and nestlings when using forage harvesters and mowers, limiting the use of herbicides and pesticides to what is essential, working with small fields instead of wide prairies, managing woodlands for coppice and hardwood production instead of feeding the pulp mills with trash conifers and limiting grazing pressure to the level which the land can sustain – all and any of these things will improve the ground for shooting, for wildlife, and ultimately for all of us.

9 Syndicates

Ideally we would all like to have our own shoot, with the time and the money to run it exactly as we wished, and then be able to invite our friends to come along and enjoy their sport as our guests. There are few greater satisfactions than to sit down at the end of a shooting day knowing that things have gone well and that your guests have had good sport, whether that sport produced half a dozen walked-up grouse or half a thousand driven pheasants. In reality, it is only the fortunate few who can still offer such hospitality; many – perhaps most – of us enjoy our shooting as part of a syndicate.

There are many possible permutations for the structure and organisation of a syndicate shoot, but they can mostly be placed in one of two general categories: the managed syndicate where a landowner, sporting agent or shoot manager runs the shoot and lets out the shooting by the day or by the season; and the shoot co-operative, where the guns themselves are the organisers, and very often the workforce as well. Our concern here is primarily with the latter set-up, although much of what applies to the co-operative syndicate will also be true for a managed syndicate shoot. And of course, a shoot may not fall neatly

Most guns will appreciate a few minutes to get organised before moving off to the first drive.

A walking gun in line with the beaters as they work through young forestry planting.

into one category or the other, since many let syndicates will involve a degree of co-operative management from their members.

In a completely managed syndicate the owner or his agent is likely to decide the number of birds to be released, the number of shooting days, the number of guns and – within broad limits – the number of birds to be shot on each day. The guns' involvement will begin when they agree to the terms set out in the syndicate agreement and end with the shoot. Everything else – keepering, shoot day organisation, budgeting and financial control – will be the responsibility of the shoot manager.

For many guns this is the ideal arrangement, since they can participate in their sport without having to commit their time and energy to the shoot outside of shooting days. But it is an expensive way to shoot, since someone else will have had to do all the work behind the scenes, and that work will have to be paid for out of the shoot fees. For those who prefer to have a closer involvement with the organisation of their sport, or who perhaps cannot afford to pay the price of a managed syndicate, the co-operative syndicate may offer a better solution.

There are many possible permutations of responsibilities within a syndicate. At one extreme there could be sixteen or so guns sharing all the work of the shoot between them: rearing, releasing and feeding the birds, controlling vermin, organising shoot days, ordering poults and food, paying the rent, arranging beaters and pickers up, keeping the shoot's accounts and even, in the larger syndicates, taking turns to act as beaters. At the other end of the scale two or three members might get together to finance and manage the shoot, possibly employing a professional keeper to do the bulk of the day-to-day work, and then let out the remaining places to guns who are simply there to shoot. In between these extremes you can adopt any variation you might wish to try.

The advantages and the disadvantages of forming and running a syndicate shoot are fairly clear. The more guns there are involved in the syndicate the lower the unit price per gun will be for any particular level of sport. It may cost £16,000 per season to rent a shoot, stock it with 2,500 pheasant poults and feed them, pay a part-time keeper, beaters and pickers up and meet all the other incidental costs of the shoot. You might meet all the costs yourself, and for your money you might be able to shoot eight days per season with eight guns and average 125 birds each day. If you were shooting yourself each day you would be able to invite seven friends on each of the eight days and hopefully have a thoroughly good time throughout the season.

But that would depend on your having £16,000 to spare to spend on shooting. Alternatively, you might split the costs equally with seven other guns and pay £2,000 per head for your shooting. You would not be able to invite all your friends along, but with luck most of your fellow syndicate members would already be – or would become – friends.

If £2,000 per head is a little steep you might decide to share some of the work throughout the season as well as the actual shooting. If your poults, rent and food was costing £10,000 and the rest was going towards the keeper's wages, the beaters and the pickers up, you could decide to pay just £1,250 per head, do the keepering yourselves and 'pay' the beaters by giving them a keeper's day at the end of the season when they could shoot while you and the regular guns acted as beaters.

As we saw in Chapter 2, if that is still a little bit expensive, you could double the size of the syndicate and take it in turns to shoot and beat on alternate drives. This would mean that £625 apiece would still give you eight shooting days, except that you would only be standing on alternate drives. You would have to buckle down and do your share of the feeding, watering, ride-cutting, beating, trap-checking, fox-lamping, poacher-patrolling and all the rest of the shoot chores, but at least you would get to spend a lot of time in the open air, and you would have a much better appreciation of what goes into getting those birds to fly over your gun when you next attend a managed driven shoot.

There are two major advantages to forming a working syndicate. The obvious one is that you reduce the cost of your shooting. The less obvious one is that you will have a much closer involvement with the day-to-day problems of running a shoot. If all you can see is a lot of hard work for no reward then you are probably not the right person to get involved in a working syndicate. If, however, you enjoy working with your hands, have a deeper interest in shooting than simply firing a gun on shoot days, take pleasure from being out in the countryside even when the weather is bad and are prepared to take your fair share of the dirty jobs as well as the fun ones, then you are probably just the person to sign up.

It is important to understand right from the beginning that there are two kinds of people who join working syndicates. There are the ones who are willing to work and the ones who are willing to let them. In my experience about half the members of any syndicate will fall into each category. Half will turn up prepared to get stuck in and do their share on a working party; the other half will attend only when they cannot get out of it and will probably not be much use even when they do turn up. The same will be true of your rotas for checking traps, feeding and watering the poults in the release pen, topping up hoppers and watching for poachers. Some will perform these tasks conscientiously; others will only work under duress and close supervision.

Most syndicates will have one or two determined 'skivers' who will always have an excuse for not turning out on work days, missing their turn at checking traps, not visiting the release pen or letting their hoppers run dry. Most syndicates will also have a few treasures who can be relied upon to do more than their fair share, whatever the weather and whatever other demands are made on their time. In between, there will be the rest of the members, who will work quite satisfactorily provided that they are given the occasional nudge. It is at this point that the role of a good shoot captain or manager becomes vital.

If too many of your members are never seen except on shooting days you may find that even the better workers become reluctant to put in maximum effort. The initial enthusiasm of the first season or two will soon wear off, and it quickly becomes obvious that a few of the syndicate members are having to work disproportionately hard in order to carry the rest. This is particularly galling if one of those who will not work starts to complain about a shortage of birds in the drives or a lack of properly cleared rides in the coverts. You might think that someone who has failed to put in their fair share of the work would have more sense than to complain about the quality of the work done by the rest of the syndicate, but you would be wrong. And unless something is done about it the willing workers may become less willing until a snowball effect means that nothing at all gets done.

You will not get any work out of the real 'skivers', no matter what you try. The answer is either to replace them in the syndicate with someone who will do their share of the work or to introduce some system of fines for those who do not turn up for work parties and routine jobs. This might be more palatable if it is couched in terms of a rebate for working, repayable at the end of the season subject to a certain amount of work being carried out. Alternatively, you could have a two-tier system of subscription, with the guns allowed to choose between paying a lower fee and undertaking a share of the shoot duties, or paying more money in order to be a shooting member only. Provided you do not have too many drones among your workers this can work well and stem the resentment that can otherwise mar the shoot.

The real enthusiasts will be there anyway, getting on with whatever needs doing without being ordered or organised. It is the rest – those who *will* stand their turn on the rota, *will* attend working days, *will* keep their hoppers properly topped up *provided* that someone organises them properly – who will make the difference between success and failure for a co-operative syndicate. None of your syndicate members will have to be telephoned on

Even if you plant conifers you may still end up with mixed woodland due to natural regeneration.

the evening before a shoot day to remind them to attend. Memory is a somewhat selective thing. You will find that syndicate members who will turn up like clockwork on every shoot day with no reminder after the initial arrangement, say, to shoot every other Saturday, starting on 28 October will somehow be subject to alarming memory lapses where the working day everyone discussed the previous week is concerned. Members who will let you know in advance if they are going to miss a shoot day, and religiously send a substitute along in their place, will completely forget an appointment to cut the reeds on a flight pond or to brash the rides in a wood. It is a little understood medical phenomenon but it is nonetheless true. If you want a full team out on work days you will have to nudge them and nag them near the day in order to ensure that they remember to turn up.

In the same way it is essential that the arrangements for the routine feeding of poults and filling of wheat hoppers are clearly understood by everyone. If the task of keeping all the feeders full is vaguely shared by all the guns you will either find two or three of your members turning out week after week to do all the work, or you will find empty hoppers – and empty coverts – on shoot days. Probably you will end up with a combination of the two – some coverts regularly fed, others only attended to intermittently. If visiting the poults in the release pen is not arranged on a properly organised rota the odds are that your poults will be fending for themselves on several days per week. If the day that someone fails to visit coincides with the day that the electric fence leads become detached from the battery you may pay heavily for that failure when a passing fox finds the temporary gap in your defences.

If you are going to run a working syndicate involving more than two or three members you must, unless you are very lucky with your members, have someone organising the work rotas, agreeing the divisions of responsibility with the members and then checking, reminding, nagging and harrying to ensure that everyone pulls their weight. You will probably still have the odd drone who must be carried, but if the rest of the members are gently reminded or cajoled, they will generally turn to and do their share of the work. You cannot realistically hope for much more.

There are a number of key areas of work that must be organised if a shoot is to run smoothly and successfully. The obvious tasks such as looking after the poults in the release pens, feeding the hoppers in the coverts, putting down straw rides, setting up sewelling, dogging in birds when they start to wander, lamping foxes, setting and checking traps and snares and generally keeping an eye open for poachers, vandals and the like may be shared among the syndicate members or they may be the responsibility of a keeper – a full-time or part-time professional, or even a keen amateur. Those tasks obviously have to be agreed among the members or there will be nothing to shoot. It is the other, less obvious, jobs that can make the difference between a shoot that runs smoothly and amicably and one which simply stumbles from crisis to crisis.

Let us first consider the tasks. Subscriptions must be collected and banked. Bills must be checked and paid. Some of the members will need reminding of the due date for paying their fees, and there should be at least some rudimentary bookkeeping so that money flowing in and out of the syndicate is accounted for. If the syndicate is run as a co-operative then a simple set of accounts should be prepared and circulated at the end of each season. Poults (or chicks or eggs) will have to be priced and ordered, and the delivery will have to be co-ordinated so that the release pens are ready to receive them when they arrive. Food and straw must be ordered, delivery or collection arranged, and labour organised to

Using a radio to co-ordinate guns and beaters.

*A gun sharing a joke
with pickers up at the end
of a drive.*

help offload and store it. Someone must keep an eye on food stocks and reorder in plenty of time if more is needed.

Someone must negotiate and pay for the shooting lease if you do not own the rights yourselves, and this may require you to file a return of all the game and vermin shot each year. If you shoot enough birds someone may need to make arrangements for the surplus to be sold through a game dealer; price and delivery or collection arrangements will have to be agreed, and a check kept to ensure that the correct payments are made when due.

The guns should be properly notified, in writing, of shoot dates, times and venues, and of any changes. Beaters and pickers up must be contacted, booked and paid for their labour if that is your arrangement. If you supply a shoot lunch the catering must be organised; if you lunch at a local pub or hotel, a booking must be made and the bill paid. If you have an end-of-season dinner the venue must be booked, the numbers who will attend ascertained and perhaps an after-dinner speaker organised.

On shoot days there should be a shoot captain who will agree, with the keeper, if you have one, which drives are to be shot and in what order. Someone must run the beating line, place any stops or pickers up and arrange for wounded birds to be picked between drives or at the end of the day. Ideally you should have two 'field marshals', one organising the beaters, the other sorting out the guns, placing them in the correct spots, warning them if there is a hidden stop or a neighbouring gun at a potentially dangerous angle, reminding everyone of the safety precautions required and of any local shoot rules, arranging the draw for pegs and seeing that everyone is numbering correctly for each drive.

Then there is the equipment. The release pens must be erected and maintained, the feeders and drinkers have to be built or bought, as do the crow cages and Larsen traps, electric fence units and Fenn traps. If you are fortunate you may have someone in the syndicate with the necessary skills and time, who is willing to undertake the routine maintenance of the shoot equipment and build new pen sections, cage traps, feeders and the like when they are needed.

In summary, there are a number of different skills required to run a shoot, and to run it smoothly and successfully. There is a need for an administrator-cum-accountant who will see to the paperwork – collecting subscriptions and paying bills, ordering supplies and issuing reminders of shoot days, work days and the like. There is a need for someone to organise the day-to-day running of the shoot – the keepering side of things, which may be done by a specialist or shared collectively among some or all of the syndicate members. There should be proper organisation on shoot days with the drives planned in advance and with clear lines of responsibility known to everyone taking part. If you allow a shoot day to be organised by general discussion between drives your shoot will quickly descend into anarchy.

It may be that all of the above tasks are undertaken by the same person in your shoot. The person who organises the paperwork may also be the one who does the keepering, runs the shoot days and organises the annual dinner. If so, and if it works satisfactorily, then fine; why interfere with a successful system? However, if you are setting up a new syndicate or reorganising an existing one, it may be worthwhile spending a little time looking at the jobs you need done and trying to match them to the people best suited to carry them out. If you have a syndicate member who has good links to the local farming community, and who has a particular knack for negotiating a good price, then he is surely the one to order in your poults, wheat and straw, and if you have an accountant on the strength then let him keep the shoot books – provided in both cases that they are willing to take on the task.

The most important thing is that anyone who is doing a job knows, and accepts, that that job is his responsibility. It is no good having a half-agreed arrangement with someone that he 'might be able to get the poults a bit cheaper this season'. If you do that without clear confirmation you will either end up with no poults at all because everyone assumed that someone else had ordered them, or because the person concerned thought he was only going to order them if he could get the right deal, or you will find you have double your requirements and no money left to pay for their food.

I think the ideal syndicate management team would consist of three or four people. One

Using the headboard of the beater's trailer as a game cart.

would handle all the paperwork, one would organise the physical side of the work and two would work together to run beaters and guns on a shooting day. The most important thing is that you try and pick people who are suited to their particular tasks, and that everyone knows exactly who is responsible for which aspect of the shoot. A vague division of responsibilities combined with a general expectation that people will turn up and do their bit without being requested or reminded may work in the first season or so but it is unlikely to work for very long. People are not like that.

In the end, while it is a pleasure to be a member of a well-organised and efficiently run syndicate, a badly run syndicate is just not worth the effort. Most people will get stuck in and do their fair share of the work provided that they are given the right encouragement, and once they have been nagged into turning out many will find that they quite enjoy doing something useful for once in a while.

No two syndicates are exactly alike, and the way in which you set yours up will depend on the type of shoot you are running, the geographical distribution of your syndicate members and their individual nature. It is the final point that is the most important, and it is on that the success of the whole enterprise rests.

10 Shooting

So far we have spent a lot of time looking at the background work and planning that has to be done in order to run a shoot. No matter how large or small your aspirations, no matter whether you hope to shoot ten head of game or 10,000 in your first season, unless your intention is simply to walk around your ground and shoot at whatever happens to get up, you will have laid your plans and carried out some of the work before the morning of the first shoot day. What happens in the next few hours will determine whether your work and planning has been worthwhile – whether the project has been a success.

But how can you begin to judge whether a shooting day has been a success? The amount of game shot may give an indication, but only if you also know the number that the guns were expected to shoot. We shot sixty pheasants in a single day on three occasions last season and reckoned it a great success because normally we would consider between forty and fifty to be a good day. If our neighbours across the valley had shot sixty on any day the keeper would probably have been scanning the situations vacant columns and glancing nervously over his shoulder, because on an average day they shoot around 300.

We were once working the dogs for a team of guns in the north of Scotland and I returned to the game larder on 12 August with seven brace in my gamebag. We had walked over the hills for around seven hours in glorious weather, the dogs had worked well, the guns had shot well and we were all delighted with that seven brace. On the same day our host had been shooting driven grouse on a moor a few miles to the south. His team ended the day in deepest gloom, and returned to their homes with all shooting cancelled for the rest of the season. Their bag, just like ours, was seven brace. The difference was primarily in our expectations for the day. We had hoped to shoot a few grouse and had done just that; they had hoped to shoot 100 brace and had not. Numbers are sometimes a useful guide to sport but they are certainly not the only yardstick by which to measure it.

Would you rather shoot half a dozen good high pheasants on a glorious December day with a rime of frost on the hedges, a stiff breeze to make them curl and a friendly crowd of guns and beaters to join in the crack at lunch, or would you prefer to shoot fifty soggy flappers on a wet and miserable November day when walking 20 yards leaves you with 10 pounds of mud on each boot and the makings of a double hernia? Would you prefer to stand all day in a series of grouse butts, feeding the midges, firing the occasional cartridge and eventually shoot six birds from eight drives, or would you rather spend the day following a brace of pointers across the hill, walking 10 miles and ending up with the same six birds in your gamebag? I do not know, but I am quite certain which appeals to me. Numbers may be important, but they are not a reliable guide to the value of a day's shooting.

All sorts of different factors go into making a success of a shooting day. The weather

Grouse shooting in Sutherland on a typical Highland sporting estate.

obviously plays an important part as far as the comfort of the participants is concerned, and can also be the deciding factor in the quality of the sport. Wet, soggy pheasants rarely fly well, and grouse in a gale may be so jumpy that they are up and away as soon as the dog points them. Of course, if you are driving grouse and the wind blows a gale in the right direction, you may be able to enjoy some remarkably sporting shooting, although in that case the numbers in the bag may not be the best guide to the quality of sport. On the other hand, conditions that cause grouse to sit tightly are ideal for shooting over dogs but not so good if you are trying to drive them over the butts. Weather that is heaven for a wildfowler may be hell for a driven pheasant shot.

But although the number of birds in the bag cannot tell the whole tale of a day out shooting, nor can any other single, quantifiable factor. I know several guns who make a special point of counting the number of shots they fire and the number of birds they kill so that they can work out a kills-to-cartridges ratio every time they shoot. A lot of us make a half-hearted attempt to do something similar out of idle curiosity – I suspect quite a lot of guns keep a count of cartridges fired while things are going well but lose interest after a few double misses – but there is a danger that keeping up a good average becomes almost the whole reason for shooting. I can think of at least one keen shot who will not raise his gun to the more difficult birds because they might spoil his average. That is his choice of course, but personally I think it is taking the whole thing a lot too seriously.

There is another shoot, a long way from where I live today, in which the actual shooting is primarily a way of building up a thirst while waiting for the pub to open. All shooting stops once the bolts are drawn on the doors of the village inn, and in most cases that is the end of outdoor sports for the day. I do not know how those people measure the success of a day out with a dog and a gun, but I doubt whether it has anything to do with

A pheasant dead in the air for this gun on a rough shoot.

cartridges fired or birds in the bag. It probably has more to do with the company in the bar afterwards, and if that is how they like to spend the bulk of their shooting day then who am I to say they should do things differently?

If you are running a commercial shoot then the measure of success might be that your customers shot safely, shot well enough to make the contracted bag, paid their dues promptly and in full, and made another booking. I can think of one or two keepers whose main means of assessing the worth of a day is the value of the tips in their pockets at the end of it. There was one occasion when we worked dogs for a shooting party of such spectacular ineptness that I considered the day a great success when it ended without a dog or a human being shot. It ended without many birds being shot either, but that was incidental. There were plenty of cartridges fired, they even managed to kill a couple of exceptionally unlucky grouse, and the guns themselves were happy. The dogs and I were just relieved.

Personally, I think the only way to measure success is to ask yourself at the end of the day, whether you, your guests, your fellow guns, beaters, dog-handlers and pickers up have enjoyed the day. If they have, and you have, and if you can return home tired but content, then it has been a good day.

Now, having said that it is almost impossible to quantify the success of a shooting day, I am going to try and do just that. It is not that I believe that the number of birds shot is in any way a measure of the success of a shoot when trying to assess the worth of a day in the field, but it may be a fair reflection on the success of your shoot *management*. If you put 1,000 pheasant poults to wood and only manage to shoot perhaps twenty or thirty on a driven day which takes in the majority of your coverts, then the odds are that there is something wrong. It may be that the birds have wandered off because of a lack of food or

Rough shooting during the course of a field trial for hunt, point and retrieving breeds.

A high pheasant on a crisp, wintry morning is sure to please both guns and shoot organisers.

because the ground is unsuitable to hold them. Perhaps you have been poached, suffered huge losses to vermin, had some form of disease in the poults or simply failed to flush them because of thick cover and a lack of trained dogs. It may be that the birds are there in plenty and it is the accuracy of the guns that is at fault. It is likely that you will start your shooting day with at least an idea of the amount of game you expect to find, and in shoot *management* terms, if you end the day without your hopes being realised, for whatever reason, the day has not been a success.

It may be that your guns have thoroughly enjoyed themselves, in which case *their* day has certainly been a success. If I can spend a day shooting grouse over the pointers and come home with ten brace in the game bag I will almost certainly consider that my day has been well spent. If that day has been spent on an estate where the grouse are little more than a sideshow to the main activity of deer stalking, then the keeper will probably be delighted to see twenty full hooks in the game larder. But if it has taken place on an estate where driven days of 200 brace are commonplace, then the keeper will probably be reaching for the phone to cancel the shooting for the rest of the season. In both cases I will probably regard the day as a success, but the keeper's criteria will be different.

Numbers in the bag can be deceptive for another reason. Suppose you took a first-class team of guns to a driven pheasant shoot, put 200 birds over them of which they shot 100, expending 250 cartridges in the process. How would that compare with a day when another team of considerably less expert guns had 2,000 birds driven over them, fired 1,000 cartridges and ended up with the same number – 100 – in the bag? Which team of guns has had the better day? It depends how you measure it. The first team will certainly have a superior kills-to-cartridges ratio. On the other hand, the second team will have had a lot more shooting, and will probably have been delighted on the one time in ten when they did manage to connect. If this happened to be the first day's shooting of the season, and the same guns were coming back for seven more driven days, then it is also clear which team would go home the happier at the prospects for the rest of the season.

So there are at least two ways to measure the success of your shoot. The first, and arguably the more important, is whether, at the end of the day or of the season, those who have taken part in the shooting are happy with their sport. It does not matter whether you put down 1,000 poults and shot 100, or whether you put down 200 and shot 150; if you and your fellow guns have gone home happy at the end of every day – or even most days – then the shoot has been a success. You might like to look at ways of becoming more efficient, saving costs or improving the holding cover in your coverts, or you might think of releasing more birds – or fewer – next season. But if you can honestly say that you have enjoyed your sport then, in one respect, the shoot has been a success.

You can also define success in more quantifiable terms. If you are running a grouse shoot, or indeed any shoot which relies entirely on wild birds to provide the sport, then the number of birds on the ground will be an important measure. You may not shoot any birds at all, particularly if you are trying to resurrect a grouse moor, but if you can see a definite rise in the numbers of birds on the ground following a season of heather-burning, predator control and perhaps the supply of grit, then you are likely to consider the season successful. If you have designed and built a new release pen, planted a new covert, put in an extra block of game crop or dug out a flight pond, and the birds have taken to it as you *Shooting should be fun.*

hoped, then that part of the shoot management has been a success.

The more 'management' a shoot requires the more likely it is that the end of the season will see an attempt being made to produce some kind of balance sheet for it. If you have a rough shoot and spend your shooting days bolting rabbits, decoying pigeons or walking up the odd wild pheasant, snipe or woodcock, then there is little need to start juggling figures at the end of the season. You will know whether you have enjoyed your season or not, and whether the pleasure you derived from your shooting justified the expense. But if you bought in several thousand pheasant and partridge poults, spent a great deal of money on food, labour and equipment, and expended a lot of time organising shooting days, it is entirely proper that you should sit down at the end of the season and start asking whether it was all worthwhile.

If the shoot is your business, then the measure of success may be plain to see in the bottom line of a profit and loss account. Even if profit is not one of your objectives you will probably be wondering if your money was well spent: whether you could produce better sport for the same outlay, or the same sport for less. The end of the season is obviously the time to find the answers. However, I would suggest that the proper time to pose the questions is much earlier, before the season has even begun. In short, if you are to judge the success of the shoot at the conclusion of the season, you should really have started out with a set of objectives against which you can measure results at the end.

Before you do anything with your shoot, before you order a single poult, plan the site of a release pen or consider where best to drive your birds, you should first consider what sort of shooting you want to enjoy. It is all too easy to get into a spiral of rearing and releasing, building pens and planting game crop, advertising for guns and recruiting beaters, organising driven days and sharing your shooting with eight or nine other guns when what you would really like to do is to just rough around with a dog and shoot a couple of birds for the pot as and when the mood takes you.

The fact that you have a piece of ground that could produce a dozen drives with 1,000 birds in each drive does not mean that you have to get your order in for 12,000 poults and start constructing a dozen big release pens. You may have a moor that would lend itself to three or four driven days, producing perhaps fifty brace per day on average, but it does not follow that you *must* arrange three or four days of grouse driving. You might prefer to shoot your 150 or so brace over dogs, and have perhaps fifteen days of ten brace apiece spread over the season instead – and it would be a very sensible choice too, in my opinion. The shoot should be what you want it to be: not what someone else thinks it should be, or could be – unless, of course, that someone else is a partner in the shoot. Then you need to do some negotiating.

I am a member of a small syndicate which shoots on eight days each season, averaging under forty head per day. It is good fun, we (nearly) all muck in to share the work, and I thoroughly enjoy it. However, if I happened to control the shooting myself and did not have anyone else to consider, I would much prefer to spend my shooting time in roughing about with the spaniel in the woods and putting a few pens of partridges down so that we could shoot over the pointers on the open fields during September and October. But: as I am simply one of sixteen members of the syndicate, I go driven pheasant shooting with the rest, and very good sport it is too most of the time.

Shooting is a general term which covers a whole range of different activities. Driven pheasant shooting can be an almost sedentary occupation for the guns, with little exercise

A keeper and guns discussing tactics for the next drive.

required beyond driving from peg to peg. It is not always that way – there are plenty of driven pheasant shoots that will demand at least a modicum of fitness from the guns – but by and large the gun who enjoys exercise is likely to be better served by some other form of shooting. At the opposite end of the spectrum is walking up grouse or shooting them over bird dogs. A day on the hill after grouse could mean that you would have to walk for six or eight hours over rough ground, carrying a gun, cartridges, a coat, your lunch, your game bag and anything that you happen to shoot in the course of your walk. In between the two extremes are various forms of rough shooting, walking up snipe or partridges, flighting ducks at dawn or dusk, wildfowling on the foreshore and various other forms of the sport, some more sedentary and some more active.

In a lot of cases you will have little choice as to how you work your shoot. If you have a grouse moor which does not have a big enough stock for a driven shoot then you will be walking after them, with or without some sort of pointing dog, or leaving them alone. If you are one member of a syndicate and the others are all dedicated driven shots you are going to shoot driven pheasants, no matter what your personal preference might be. If you are lucky enough to be starting from scratch, however, and have what could be termed a 'greenfield site' to work on, you might like to sit down for a while and think about how you would most like to spend your shooting days before you make any real plans about the future of the shoot.

In many ways, the more you organise your shooting the more restrictive it will become. Suppose you have a shooting lease on 1,000 acres of low ground, not very much money to invest in shooting and no wish to run a commercial operation. If you put down 100 or so pheasant poults you will probably be able to buy them, house them and feed them for about £500 – less if you are able to collect eggs and rear your own chicks instead of buying

Deep in the woods with every chance of a woodcock.

poults. Those 100 birds, or as many of them as survive to adulthood, should be enough to allow you as many days' rough shooting as you and your dog can manage, provided that you are content with shooting just a bird or two for the pot each time you go out. If you enjoy a good walk, the chance of a rabbit, a snipe or a woodcock, and a few hours in the country rather than standing at a peg and firing off a pocket full of cartridges while someone else does the hard work, then you may have created the ideal shoot – for you.

Since you are the sole proprietor of the shoot you will be able to wander about whenever the fancy takes you, to take a friend or two along if you wish, and to shoot as many or as few birds as you want and are able to find in any one day. But suppose that you decide instead to invite seven or eight friends to join you in the shoot, to put in £500 apiece so that you can buy 1,000 poults instead of 100, and organise eight or nine days driven shooting. You will have a lot more birds about the place, but in fairness to the rest of the syndicate you will no longer be able to enjoy a day's shooting just whenever you please. You have a collective responsibility now, and shooting will probably have to be reserved for regular shoot days only. You may get more shooting for your money, but you will also lose a lot of the freedom and spontaneity that you enjoyed before.

You may prefer the more formal style of a driven shoot. You may enjoy the company, the lunch-time banter and the more testing shooting that good driven birds will offer. You may not like walking all day, fighting your way through thorns and brambles while trying to control a wild spaniel or persuade a fat labrador to get out and hunt. You may not have the time or inclination to spend your summer nurturing pheasant chicks and carrying wheat out to the release pens. The freedom and spontaneity that appeals to me may have little attraction for you, and your viewpoint is every bit as valid as mine.

The most important thing to understand about shooting is that we do it because we enjoy it. If we simply wanted to eat pheasants we could rear them intensively in a broiler house, feed them on the same mixture of recycled offal, growth hormones, antibiotics and live vaccines that our chickens are offered and pump the carcasses full of phosphates after they had been 'humanely' killed by being hung from a shackle and having their throats cut so that they could bleed to death. Then, after a few decades of selective inbreeding we would be producing pheasants as bland and tasteless as the frozen chickens that our supermarkets sell today. Indeed, if some of our politicians have their way that is the only type of pheasant that may be available in a few years from now. It will be all right though, because those who are rearing, killing, packaging and marketing the pheasants will take no pleasure from it – except when they count their money. There will not be a lot of pleasure in eating them either.

But we go shooting because we enjoy it. Shooting should be fun, a shooting day should be a treat to look forward to, not a duty to be fulfilled. Nor is it something to be ashamed of: hunting is a basic human instinct, and until very recently in man's evolution it was the skill of the hunters that kept the rest of the human tribe alive. I have no wish to force my values on to anyone else; I enjoy shooting – and fishing and deer stalking – but others who do not, are perfectly entitled not to become involved – provided that they do not try and force me to give up my enjoyment.

I shoot because I enjoy it. If I stop enjoying it I will stop shooting. In the meantime, I hope to be allowed to carry on, hopefully putting a little more into the shoot than I take out of it, and doing a little bit to make the countryside a better place for wildlife – and not just grouse, partridges and pheasants. I hope that you enjoy your shooting as much.

Bibliography

While shooting and fishing have occupied a great deal of my outdoor life for as long as I care to remember, I have probably spent as much time – and possibly more – at home reading about the sport. Indeed, although I can envisage a time when I will no longer be able to shoot, whether through old age or Act of Parliament, I find it hard to imagine life without books.

Reading has been one of the great joys of my life ever since I was old enough to figure out the words on a printed page. One of the first books I can remember reading was *Two Little Savages*, followed shortly afterwards by *The Land of Footprints*, the story of an African safari. My reading habits, like my other main interests in life, were set at an early age. Since then I have devoured every book I could lay my hands on regarding field sports – shooting, fishing, stalking and big-game hunting – as well as any number of novels which dealt with sport either peripherally or as their central theme. Some were excellent, others less so, and some – particularly some of the works of fiction – so spectacularly inaccurate in their treatment of their subject as to be worthy of note for that point alone. Inevitably, there are a number of authors whose work I particularly favour – generally for the quality of their writing rather than for the content *per se*. Equally, there are some whose books are hard work for me, again, usually less of because of what they say than for the way in which they say it. This is, of course, a purely subjective judgement, since a writer whose style I find particularly turgid might well be someone else's favourite author.

In compiling a bibliography after writing a book such as this it is impossible to acknowledge every author and every work which has played a part in forming my opinions about shooting and the countryside, nor every source of the ideas and suggestions that I have made with regard to running your shoot. When I say, for example, that one should set a fox wire a certain height above the ground, I have no idea whether I first learned the correct height from a book or whether I found it out by trial and error, whether I was shown the proper settings by one of the keepers I knew or whether I simply observed fox wires *in situ* and copied them later without conscious thought.

Ideas about sportsmanship and the general philosophy of shooting also come from reading, conversation, observation and simply considering what I think is good and bad in field sports today. A century ago a writer could express the opinion that '...the little owl is an unmitigated pest and should be shot at every opportunity. The country would be well rid of it.' Today it is possible to be taken to task for advising the killing of a rat, never mind anything as photogenic as a fox. I once read tales of hunters shooting elephant and lion, rhino and leopard and was invited to admire their bravery and resourcefulness. Now an elephant cull is regarded as a necessary evil by some and a sin against nature by others. Even so, I can still read those old tales and admire the men that did the deeds and lived to write about them, even if I no longer share their philosophy of life and death.

I cannot therefore provide a list of every book and every author on whom I may have drawn, consciously or subconsciously, when preparing this work. However, there are a number of books which I have found particularly useful at one time or another, and I will list them here in the hope that they may also be of use to you.

Partridge For Sport by Geoffrey Nightingale (Boydell and Brewer 1990) was of considerable help when we first started our hill partridge experiment. There is plenty of old literature about partridge keepering, but there seems to be very little that is strictly relevant to modern farming and the release pen methods which we had to adopt. The Euston system may be an excellent way of producing partridges if you have a full team of keepers and ample time to devote to it, but it is hardly relevant for the do-it-yourself shoot where no wild partridges exist to begin with.

Your Shoot by Ian McCall (A & C Black 1985) is an excellent and comprehensive guide to nearly all aspects of running and keepering a low-ground shoot. The author has enjoyed a long association with the Game Conservancy and writes with great authority, but in an easy-to-follow and refreshingly jargon-free style. I have already mentioned the Game Conservancy several times and will do so again now. They do a superb job, not only in carrying out scientifically validated research into a myriad of aspects of field sports, but in actively aiding and advising shoot owners, managers and gamekeepers. Their magazine and yearbook are themselves worth the annual subscription, and a visit from one of their area advisors can be invaluable in helping you to set up your shoot on sound principles right from the beginning.

Fair Game by Charlie Parkes and John Thornley (Pelham Books 1987) is a useful reference work for all aspects of the law as it applies to shooting and field sports in general. It is not exactly bedside reading, but it does contain both the detail of the various Acts governing field sports and the countryside and easily understood summaries of the implications of the legal jargon.

The Fox and the Orchid by Robin Page (Quiller Press 1987) will tell you very little about the mechanics of running a shoot, but it does give an excellent insight into the world of field sports through the eyes of a farmer and countryman who is not himself a participant in shooting, hunting or fishing. It is a good read for anyone who enjoys field sports and should be compulsory reading for every one of our Members of Parliament, and particularly those who are opposed to country sports. Sadly, those who would most benefit from this well-researched, cogently argued and entertainingly written work are probably the very people who are least likely to read it – and most likely to be vociferous in support of any Bill to ban hunting, fishing and shooting.

The Fur, Feather and Fin Series (first published in the 1890s, but recently reprinted by the Signet Press) is a twelve-volume series of books covering, among other species, pheasants, partridges, grouse, hares, snipe and woodcock, salmon, trout, red deer, foxes and wildfowl. Written by the foremost authorities of the day, they provide a fascinating insight into the attitudes and methods used to preserve game and organise shooting at the turn of the century. Much of the advice is still relevant today, although not those parts which deal with predator control.

There are many, many other books which I have read and enjoyed. *The Amateur Keeper* by Major Archie Coats is one. It is a particularly useful book if you happen to be running a shoot on a small area. John Humphreys has written, and continues to write, a number of books covering wildfowling, rough shooting, pigeon shooting and shoot management, all of which are both entertaining and educational. If you can find a copy of *The Old Man and the Boy* by Robert Ruark then buy it; it is a beautifully written story and sets out the whole philosophy of country sports in a manner which will appeal to both the committed sportsman and the interested bystander. The books by 'BB' (Denys Watkins-Pitchford), Colin Willock, Colin McKelvie, Keith Erlandson, Lea MacNally, J. K. Stanford, Gough Thomas and perhaps a dozen others have all enthused and educated me, shaped my attitudes to shooting and fishing, and entertained me in my spare moments for many, many years. I hope they, and others, will continue to do so for many years to come.

Index